YESTERDAY
AND
TODAY

From the Kitchens of

STOKELY-VAN CAMP

A Benjamin Company Book

Cover photo: *Eastern Beans with Pork Chops (page 97), Green Beans with Bacon Dressing (page 120), Orange Glazed Beets (page 113), Colonial Pot Roast (page 46), Corn Muffins (page 148), Vegetable Pepperoni Salad (page 126), Coffee Peach Parfaits (page 169), Orangey Pumpkin Bread (page 147)*

Copyright © 1980 Stokely-Van Camp, Inc.,
and The Benjamin Company, Inc. All rights reserved.

Published by The Benjamin Company, Inc.
485 Madison Avenue
New York, N.Y. 10022

ISBN: 0-87502-071-2

Library of Congress Catalog Card Number: 79-54945

Printed in the United States of America

Table of Contents

The Story of Stokely-Van Camp   5

Helpful Hints   6

The Light Touch
    Appetizers and Snacks   7

Quick Fillers
    Soups, Sandwiches and Easy Fixin's   19

The Heart of the Meal
    Main Dishes   35

To Complement the Meal
    Vegetables   89

Serve It Cold
    Salads and Dressings   125

Special Treats
    A Potpourri of Surprises   141

Festive Finale
    Desserts   155

Ingredient Equivalents   185

Ingredient Substitutions   186

Index   187

Greetings . . .

Have you noticed how often restaurants proclaim "home cooking" in their advertisements? That's because we know "there's no cooking like home cooking." And it's fun!

Cooking isn't difficult. It's simply a matter of putting ingredients together, adjusting flavors, gently blending, and using your tasting spoon often.   All cooks add their own special ingredient: "tender loving care." With these quality ingredients, you'll surely have a prize-winning meal.

We invite you to let the aroma of "Yesterday" drift into your kitchen "Today" with this specially selected collection of our favorites. Each recipe has been kitchen-tested just for you. Enjoy!

Good Cooking Always!

Marge Ashby

Marge Ashby
Director,
The Kitchens of Stokely-Van Camp

How it began . . .

Back in 1872, John B. Stokely and his wife, Anna, inherited a family farm near Newport, Tennessee. After Mr. Stokely's untimely death in 1890, the family of five sons and three daughters worked hard at farming and obtaining a business education. With $3,900, part of which came from a friend, Stokely Bros. & Company was established in 1898 to can tomatoes and other vegetables. The canning industry experienced great growth in the early 1900's. More plants were purchased and the general offices moved to Louisville, Kentucky.

In 1933, a most significant step was taken: the purchase of the Van Camp Packing Company in Indianapolis. Van Camp added nonseasonal food items to an established seasonal line; and in 1944, the company name was changed to Stokely-Van Camp, Inc. Soon the product line was further broadened with the addition of several frozen food operations. The company continued to grow and acquire subsidiary companies such as Pomona Products Company in Griffin, Georgia (known for their pimientos); Capital City Products Company in Columbus, Ohio (known for its oil products); M.W. Graves and Company, Ltd., in Canada (known for canned and frozen foods); and Purity Mills, Inc. in Dixon, Illinois (known for their popcorn and cereals).

One of the most revolutionary new products to come from Stokely-Van Camp is Gatorade® thirst quencher. It is known as the drink of athletes and other active people.

Today, Stokely-Van Camp, Inc., is the largest independent processor of canned and frozen foods in the United States. We are proud of our company and its fine products. We are equally proud that our top executive group includes descendants of the original Stokely family.

Helpful Hints

When grating cheese, the grater is much easier to wash if both sides of the cutting surface are first coated with vegetable oil spray.

To prevent oven drips when baking pies, put a paper collar on each pie. Cut a 1 1/2-inch-wide strip from the top of a paper bag. (Several strips may be cut from one bag.) Wet the strip of paper and remove excess moisture. Place damp strip snugly around prepared pie. Secure with paper clip. Tear off excess paper. Bake pie as usual. Remove collar as soon as paper is cool enough to handle. The collar protects the edges of the pie crust from overbrowning.

You can have the modern version of the classic stockpot: keep a plastic container in the freezer and when you have leftover vegetables and vegetable liquids, add them to the container. Use the stockpot when preparing soup.

Leftover bits of bread, ends of loaves, crackers — practically any bread product — can be turned into crumbs in a blender or food processor and stored in the freezer in a tightly covered container. Then you have instant topping for plain vegetables or a good start toward fancier dishes. Crumbs are also good as thickeners for gravies and stews.

Small bits of cheese (you can use several kinds together) will be used if they are grated and stored, tightly covered, in the refrigerator or freezer. Good for toppings, sauces, and quick appetizers.

Save margarine wrappers in the refrigerator and use for greasing pans.

A bunch of lunch ideas for brown bags, picnics, lunch buckets, or for a quick meal at home: Pop open a 7 3/4-ounce can of Van Camp's® Chilee Weenee®, Beanee Weenee®, Noodlee Weenee, Skettee Weenee, or Pork and Beans. Eat 'em cold or eat 'em hot . . . right from the can as each has a handy pull top "kwik opener" lid. Don't dirty a pan; just heat them in the can (remove label first and slightly crack lid to allow steam to escape). They're *delicious!*

Appetizers and Snacks

MINIATURE CHICKEN
EGG FOO YUNG

An appetizer with a flair.

1 package (14 ounces)
    Frozen Stokely's®
    Japanese Style
    Stir-Fry Vegetables
5 eggs
2 Tablespoons soy sauce
1 1/4 cups diced, cooked
    chicken

4 Tablespoons all-purpose
    flour
4 Tablespoons vegetable
    oil
    Chinese hot mustard
    Duck sauce

Prepare vegetables according to package directions and set aside. Beat eggs with soy sauce until frothy. Combine chicken and flour in a small bowl. Add vegetables and chicken mixture to beaten eggs and stir until well combined. Heat oil in a large skillet. Drop heaping Tablespoonfuls of mixture into hot oil to make miniature pancakes. Brown well on both sides. Drain on paper towels and keep warm. Serve with small bowls of hot mustard and duck sauce for dipping.   *4 to 6 servings*

SPINACH-CHEESE SPREAD

A cheese spread with a flair.

1 package (8 ounces)
    cream cheese
1 package (10 ounces)
    Frozen Stokely's®
    Chopped Spinach,
    thawed
3 cloves garlic, finely
    minced
1/4 cup finely minced onion
1 Tablespoon
    Worcestershire sauce
3 Tablespoons
    half-and-half
2 Tablespoons chopped
    chives
2 teaspoons lemon juice
1/8 teaspoon nutmeg
    Few drops hot pepper
    sauce

Place cream cheese in bowl of electric mixer and beat on medium speed until creamy. Drain spinach thoroughly, squeezing out as much water as possible. Add spinach, garlic, onion, Worcestershire sauce, half-and-half, chives, lemon juice, nutmeg, and hot pepper sauce to cream cheese mixture and stir until well combined. Place in attractive serving bowl, cover, and refrigerate until serving time. Serve with cocktail bread and assorted crackers.   *About 2 cups*

CHEESE FILLED BEETS

Attractive as appetizer, garnish, or salad.

1 can (16 ounces)
    Stokely's Finest®
    Tiny Whole Beets,
    well drained
1 package (3 ounces)
    cream cheese, softened
1 Tablespoon mayonnaise
1/2 teaspoon vinegar
    Dash seasoned salt
    Dash onion powder

Cut thin slice from bottom of each beet to form flat surface. Using a grapefruit spoon, melon ball cutter, or sharp knife, scoop out center of each beet. Blend remaining ingredients and stuff into beets. Arrange on lettuce leaves or serving plate for appetizers or use as garnish for meat platter.   *16 to 20 appetizers*

Note: If larger beets are used, cut beet in half and treat each half as one appetizer.

PIMIENTO CHEESE SPREAD

Stores well in refrigerator for several weeks. Great for sandwiches or tiny appetizers.

1/2 cup cider vinegar
1/2 cup milk
1 egg, beaten
2 Tablespoons sugar
1 Tablespoon plus 1 teaspoon all-purpose flour
1/8 teaspoon salt
1 cup salad dressing (mayonnaise-style)
5 jars (4 ounces each) Stokely's Finest® Sliced Pimientos, well drained
2 pounds American cheese, finely grated*

Combine vinegar, milk, egg, sugar, flour, and salt in saucepan and cook over moderate heat, stirring constantly, until mixture bubbles and thickens. Cool. Stir in salad dressing and set aside. Chop pimientos, combine with cheese and stir into prepared dressing. Spread on small slices of bread or crackers.   *8 cups*

* You can use your food processor.

MELON BALLS ON ICE

Delicious with fruit punch.

1 package (16 ounces) Frozen Stokely's® Melon Balls
1 Tablespoon butter, softened
1 package (3 ounces) cream cheese, softened
2 cups sifted confectioners sugar
1 teaspoon grated orange peel
2 Tablespoons orange juice
1/2 cup finely chopped nuts (optional)
Crushed ice

Allow melon balls to partially defrost; drain and set aside. Cream butter and cream cheese. Blend in sugar and orange peel; add orange juice and beat until smooth and creamy. Fold in nuts. Place dip in small bowl surrounded by crushed ice. Place melon balls on top of ice. Spear melon balls with cocktail picks and dunk in dip.   *4 servings*

HOT BEAN DIP

Great for a party or as a zingy accompaniment to scrambled eggs.

1 can (16 ounces)
    Van Camp's® Pork
    and Beans
2 Tablespoons minced
    pickled jalapeño pepper

4 ounces pasteurized
    process cheese spread,
    cubed
Corn chips

In blender purée pork and beans and jalapeño pepper. Pour into saucepan, add cheese and heat until cheese is melted. Garnish with additional chopped jalapeño pepper if desired. Serve with corn chips.   *About 2 cups*

Microwave Method: In blender purée pork and beans and jalapeño pepper. Pour into bowl, add cheese, cover, and microcook 2 to 3 minutes, or until cheese is melted. Stir twice. Serve with corn chips.

SPINACH BALLS

Sophisticated appetizers that make a hit!

2 packages (10 ounces
    each) Frozen Stokely's®
    Chopped Spinach
2 medium-size onions,
    chopped
6 eggs, unbeaten
2 cups herb-seasoned
    stuffing mix

1/2 cup grated Parmesan
    cheese
1/4 cup butter or margarine,
    melted
1 teaspoon salt
1 Tablespoon garlic salt
1/2 teaspoon thyme
    Pepper to taste

Preheat oven to 350°F. Thaw spinach and place in large sieve. Drain spinach thoroughly, squeezing out as much water as possible. Add spinach to remaining ingredients; mix well. Shape mixture into balls the size of walnuts. Bake on greased jelly-roll pan 20 minutes. Serve promptly.   *About 60 appetizers*

Nice to know: Spinach balls may be wrapped and frozen, then thawed 1 hour before baking.

Opposite: Hot Bean Dip, Stokely's Finest® Tomato Juice, Spinach Balls

MEATBALLS IN RED WINE SAUCE

So good they will disappear in a hurry.

1 large onion, finely chopped
1 cup fine dry bread crumbs
2 pounds lean ground beef
3 eggs
1/2 teaspoon salt
1/4 teaspoon pepper
1/2 teaspoon seasoned salt
3/4 teaspoon curry powder
1/4 cup grated Parmesan cheese
1/2 teaspoon Worcestershire sauce

2 cloves garlic, minced, divided
1 cup all-purpose flour
2 Tablespoons vegetable oil
1 cup dry red wine
1/2 cup beef consommé
2 cans (8 ounces each) Stokely's Finest® Tomato Sauce
1/8 teaspoon oregano

Combine onion, crumbs, ground beef, eggs, salt, pepper, seasoned salt, curry powder, cheese, and Worcestershire sauce plus 1 clove minced garlic; form into 1 1/2-inch meatballs. Roll lightly in flour. Place oil and remaining clove minced garlic in large skillet; add meatballs and brown over moderate heat on all sides (about 8 minutes). Meanwhile, combine remaining ingredients in large saucepan and bring to a simmer. Add meatballs and simmer about 25 to 35 minutes. Transfer to chafing dish and serve with cocktail picks.   *About 60 to 70 meatballs*

APPLESAUCE FLIP

An afternoon pick-me-up.

1 can (8 1/2 ounces) Stokely's Finest® Applesauce
1 1/2 teaspoons rum or brandy extract

3 Tablespoons sugar
2 1/4 cups milk
3 small scoops vanilla ice cream
6 crushed ice cubes

Combine all ingredients in blender; blend for 1 minute, or until very frothy.   *4 8-ounce servings*

STRAWBERRY MOCHA SHAKE

A creamy cooler.

1 package (16 ounces)
   Frozen Stokely's®
   Strawberry Halves in
   Syrup, thawed

1/2 cup hot coffee
1 teaspoon cinnamon
1 quart vanilla ice cream

Combine strawberries, coffee, and cinnamon; stir to blend. Place ice cream in container of blender and add strawberry mixture. Process on medium speed until all ice cream is blended. Pour shake into glasses.   *4 to 6 servings*

Note: To thin shake, add additional coffee.

FROTHY NECTAR

Fruity drink for a hot summer's day.

1/2 pint vanilla ice cream
1 can (8 3/4 ounces)
   Stokely's Finest®
   Fruit Cocktail,
   undrained

1 cup milk

Combine all ingredients in blender; cover and blend 30 seconds.   *3 1/2 cups*

TRIGO SHAKE

Perfect for a breakfast or snack treat.

2 cups Popeye Puffed
   Wheat
1 1/2 cups milk
1 cup crushed ice

4 Tablespoons sugar
1/2 teaspoon vanilla extract
Dash salt

Combine all ingredients in blender; cover and blend thoroughly.   *2 servings*

Nice to know: To make a Low-Cal Trigo Shake, substitute 1 1/2 cups reconstituted dry milk for 1 1/2 cups milk, and substitute 1/4 teaspoon granulated sugar substitute for 4 Tablespoons sugar.

NATURAL MUNCH

This mix is popular with all ages.

2 1/2 quarts popped Popeye
      Popcorn (about 1/3 cup
      unpopped)
   1 cup salted peanuts
   1 cup wheat germ
   1 cup sugar

1/3 cup honey
1/3 cup water
1/4 cup butter or margarine,
    melted
1/2 teaspoon salt

Preheat oven to 250°F. Grease two 15×10×1-inch jelly-roll pans. In a large greased bowl toss together popcorn, peanuts, and wheat germ. Set aside. Combine remaining ingredients in 2-quart saucepan. Cook over medium heat, stirring constantly until sugar is dissolved and mixture begins to boil. Continue cooking until mixture reaches 250°F. on candy thermometer (hard ball stage). Pour over popcorn mixture slowly, stirring to coat. Spread in prepared jelly-roll pans. Bake 45 minutes, stirring every 10 or 15 minutes. Remove from oven; stir to distribute flavor. When cool, store in tightly covered containers.   *3 quarts*

CHOCO-PEANUT BUTTER CHEWS

Let the children help make this recipe.

   1 cup sugar
   1 cup light corn syrup
1 1/2 cups peanut butter
   6 cups Popeye Puffed
      Wheat or Puffed Rice
   1 package (6 ounces)
      semi-sweet real
      chocolate morsels

1 package (6 ounces)
    artificial butter-
    scotch flavored
    morsels

Butter a 13×9×2-inch pan. Combine sugar and corn syrup; bring to a boil. Remove from heat; add peanut butter; mix until smooth. Pour over Puffed Wheat; blend well. Press into prepared pan. Melt chocolate and butterscotch over low heat or in microwave oven. Stir to blend and spread evenly over cereal mixture. Allow to stand at room temperature until set; cut into squares.   *48 small squares*

Opposite: Natural Munch, Gatorade Popsicles (page 16), Choco-Peanut Butter Chews

GATORADE POPSICLES

Children of all ages will like these healthful treats.

1 bottle (32 ounces)
   Gatorade® thirst
   quencher

Fill each popsicle mold 3/4 full with Gatorade®. Insert popsicle holder into each mold and freeze until solid. Or, freeze in small pointed paper cups (add the holder when Gatorade® begins to harden). Snap mold to release popsicles and serve immediately. *16 popsicles*

SUGAR AND SPICE POPCORN

A one-pan procedure.

1/4 cup vegetable oil
  3 Tablespoons sugar
1/4 teaspoon cinnamon
1/4 teaspoon nutmeg

1 Tablespoon light corn
   syrup
1/3 cup unpopped Popeye
   Popcorn

Generously grease cookie sheet. Use only a hand-turned popcorn popper for this recipe because all ingredients must be agitated constantly. Combine all ingredients in popper, except popcorn. Stir well and heat until bubbling. Add popcorn; cover and stir constantly over medium heat until all corn is popped. Immediately pour onto greased cookie sheet to cool.
About 2 quarts

BAKED POPCORN CRUNCH

A light, flavorful, and easy party snack.

1/2 cup butter or
   margarine
1/2 cup firmly packed brown
   sugar

3 quarts popped Popeye
   Popcorn (about 1/2 cup
   unpopped)
1 cup pecan halves

Preheat oven to 350°F. Cream butter and brown sugar together in large bowl. Mix warm popcorn with creamed mixture. Add nuts. Spread in 15×10×1-inch jelly-roll pan. Bake 8 minutes. Cool in pan. *3 quarts*

SPUN PINK-CINNAMON POPCORN

Crispy good.

2 quarts popped Popeye Popcorn (about 1/3 cup unpopped)
3/4 cup sugar
1/4 cup light corn syrup
3 Tablespoons water
1 Tablespoon red cinnamon candy

Preheat oven to 325°F. Place 2 quarts popped corn in large buttered bowl and set aside. Combine remaining ingredients in small saucepan. Heat slowly to boiling point, stirring constantly. Cook without stirring to 285°F. (soft crack stage on candy thermometer). Remove from heat at once and drizzle over popcorn, stirring to coat evenly. When well mixed, pour onto buttered cookie sheet and place in oven for about 10 minutes to crisp corn. Separate kernels when cool enough to handle.   *2 quarts*

CRISPY CARAMEL CORN

Just like State Fair!

3 1/2 quarts popped Popeye Popcorn (about 1/2 cup unpopped)
1/2 cup cocktail peanuts (optional)
1/2 cup butter or margarine
1 cup firmly packed light brown sugar
1/4 cup light corn syrup
1/2 teaspoon salt
1/2 teaspoon vanilla extract
1/4 teaspoon baking soda

Preheat oven to 250°F. Grease well a 15×10×1-inch jelly-roll pan. Place popped popcorn and peanuts in large well greased bowl. Melt butter in large heavy saucepan; stir in brown sugar, corn syrup, and salt and bring to a boil. Reduce heat and boil 5 minutes. Remove from heat and stir in vanilla and baking soda. Pour syrup over popcorn mixture and mix well. Spread on greased jelly-roll pan. Bake 1 hour, stirring every 15 minutes. Remove from oven and separate kernels when cool enough to handle. Store in tightly covered containers.   *3 1/2 quarts*

MELON "ICE RING" PUNCH

Pretty as a picture.

1 package (16 ounces)
  Frozen Stokely's®
  Melon Balls
2 bottles (32 ounces each)
  Orange Gatorade®
  thirst quencher

1 bottle (2 liters or
  about 2 quarts)
  lemon-lime carbonated
  beverage

In the bottom of a 5-cup ring mold, evenly space 12 melon balls. Add cold water to half cover the melon balls; freeze firm. When very firm add 1 cup cold water and freeze again. Continue adding water and freezing until mold is full. Ice ring mold will last about 1 hour in cold punch.

Chill Gatorade® thirst quencher and carbonated beverage. Add both to punch bowl with remaining melon balls. Give a quick stir and top with ice ring.   *32 4-ounce servings*

Soups, Sandwiches and Easy Fixin's

ORIENTAL SOUP

A very different soup.

1/2 pound ground pork	1/2 teaspoon ginger
1 Tablespoon soy sauce	8 cups chicken broth
1 large egg, beaten, divided	1 package (16 ounces) Frozen Stokely's® Vegetables Orient®
1 teaspoon salt, divided	
3 teaspoons cornstarch, divided	1/2 cup thinly sliced bamboo shoots
3 teaspoons dry sherry, divided	1 1/2 cups cooked fine noodles
1/2 pound raw shrimp, cut fine	

Combine pork, soy sauce, 1/2 beaten egg, 1/2 teaspoon salt, 1 1/2 teaspoons cornstarch and 1 1/2 teaspoons sherry. Form into marble-size balls and set aside. Combine shrimp, ginger, remaining egg, salt, cornstarch, and sherry. Shape into marble-size balls and set aside with pork balls. Bring broth to a boil; add vegetables, bamboo shoots, reserved pork and shrimp balls. Cover and simmer over low heat 25 minutes. Stir in noodles, cook until noodles are heated through and adjust seasoning.   *4 to 6 servings*

HAMBURGER VEGETABLE SOUP

A quick and hearty soup.

1 pound lean ground beef
2/3 cup chopped onion
1 can (46 ounces)
   Stokely's Finest®
   Tomato Juice
2 cans (16 ounces each)
   Stokely's Finest®
   Mixed Vegetables

2 beef bouillon cubes
1 teaspoon seasoned salt
1 teaspoon sugar

In large saucepan brown ground beef and onion; drain excess fat. Add remaining ingredients and bring to a boil. Lower heat, cover, and simmer 30 minutes.   *6 servings*

DOUBLE BEAN SOUP ITALIAN

A hearty dish for a winter night.

1 can (21 ounces)
   Van Camp's® Pork
   and Beans
1 can (15 ounces)
   Van Camp's® Butter
   Beans
1 can (16 ounces)
   Stokely's Finest®
   Stewed Tomatoes
1 can (10 1/2 ounces)
   condensed chicken
   broth, undiluted

1/2 teaspoon seasoned salt
1 teaspoon Worcestershire
   sauce
1 Tablespoon parsley
   flakes
1 Tablespoon instant
   minced onion
1/2 teaspoon Italian
   seasoning
1/8 to 1/4 teaspoon garlic
   powder

Combine all ingredients in large kettle or saucepan. Bring to boil, reduce heat, cover, and simmer 15 minutes.   *6 to 8 servings*

Microwave Method: Combine all ingredients in 2 1/2-quart casserole. Cover and microcook 6 minutes, or until heated through. Stir twice.

DILLY-CAULIFLOWER SOUP

A rich, thick soup — great for company.

1 package (10 ounces) Frozen Stokely's® Cauliflower	3 teaspoons chicken flavored bouillon
	3 cups hot water
3 Tablespoons butter or margarine	1 cup half-and-half
1/2 cup chopped onion	2 Tablespoons chopped fresh dill or
1/2 cup chopped celery	1 Tablespoon dried dill
3 Tablespoons all-purpose flour	Sprigs of fresh dill (optional)

Cook cauliflower, omitting salt; drain and coarsely chop; set aside. Melt butter in medium-size saucepan. Add onion and celery; sauté until onion is transparent. Add flour, stirring constantly. Dissolve bouillon in hot water; gradually add to saucepan. Gently stir in cauliflower. Cook over low heat 5 minutes. Add half-and-half and dill. Heat 3 minutes over low heat; do not let soup boil. Ladle into bowls and garnish with sprigs of fresh dill.   *6 8-ounce servings*

Nice to know: For a creamier soup, place about half the cooked soup in a blender. Blend until smooth; add back to remaining soup. Serve at once.

CARROT SOUP

Rich, creamy, and nutritious.

1 can (16 ounces) Stokely's Finest® Sliced Carrots, including liquid	1 Tablespoon honey
	1/4 teaspoon salt
	1/8 teaspoon pepper
2 cups water	6 ounces pasteurized process cheese spread
1 small potato, cubed	
1 Tablespoon plus 1/2 teaspoon minced onion	

Place all ingredients except cheese in saucepan and bring to a boil. Lower heat; add cheese, stirring to dissolve completely. Cover and gently simmer about 20 minutes, or until potato is cooked. Serve at once.   *4 servings*

CROCK-COOKED VEGETABLE BEEF SOUP

This is a filling and delicious classic soup.

1 package (16 ounces) Frozen Stokely's® Size Wize® Vegetables Sized for Soup	2 pounds beef shank
	3 beef flavored bouillon cubes
1 can (16 ounces) Stokely's Finest® Whole Tomatoes	1 teaspoon salt
	4 peppercorns
	3 cups water

Place all ingredients in a crock-type slow cooker and stir well. Cover and cook on low for 6 to 8 hours or on high 3 to 4 hours. *4 to 6 servings*

Nice to know: This recipe can be doubled or tripled up to the capacity of your slow cooker. Freeze extra soup for quick, easy meals at another time.

CHILI BEEF ONION SOUP

Nicely spiced and very filling.

1 pound lean ground beef	1 envelope onion soup mix
2 cans (15 ounces each) Stokely's Finest® Dark Red Kidney Beans, drained	1/2 cup beef broth
	2 Tablespoons Stokely's Finest® Chili Sauce
1 can (16 ounces) Stokely's Finest® Stewed Tomatoes	

Brown beef in skillet and drain. Transfer to large saucepan; add remaining ingredients, cover, and simmer over low heat 30 minutes, stirring occasionally. *6 servings*

Microwave method: Crumble beef in 2 1/2-quart casserole. Microcook 5 minutes, stirring after 3 minutes. Drain; add remaining ingredients, cover, and microcook 10 minutes, stirring twice during cooking.

Opposite: Crock-Cooked Vegetable Beef Soup

CORN CHOWDER

Serve with hot biscuits for a cold-day supper.

3 Tablespoons butter or
  margarine
1 cup diced cooked ham
1/2 cup chopped onion
1/2 cup chopped celery
1/2 cup chopped green or
  red pepper
2 cups chicken broth
1 cup diced potatoes
1/8 teaspoon pepper
1 1/2 cups milk

1/2 cup heavy cream
1 can (17 ounces)
  Stokely's Finest®
  Whole Kernel Golden
  Corn
1 jar (2 ounces)
  Stokely's Finest®
  Sliced Pimientos,
  drained
Paprika

Melt butter in large saucepan. Sauté ham 5 minutes and set aside. Sauté onion, celery, and green pepper until onion is transparent. Add chicken broth, potatoes, and pepper. Cover and cook over moderate heat about 20 minutes, or until potatoes are just tender. Add milk, cream, corn, reserved ham, and pimientos. Reduce heat and cook until thoroughly heated. Do not boil. Spoon into bowls and garnish each serving with paprika.   *6 servings*

PEA SOUP

Add leftover diced ham for variety.

1 can (17 ounces)
  Stokely's Finest®
  Peas
1 cup half-and-half
1/2 small onion, quartered

2 Tablespoons butter or
  margarine
1 teaspoon instant
  chicken flavored
  bouillon
Dash pepper

Combine all ingredients in blender; purée. Pour into 1 1/2-quart saucepan, cover, and heat to serving temperature. Serve with croutons if desired.   *4 servings*

Microwave Method: Combine all ingredients in blender; purée. Pour into 2-quart casserole, cover, and microcook 4 minutes, or until heated through. Stir once.

CREAMED VEGETABLE SOUP

Great for lunch.

1/2 teaspoon salt	1/2 pound bacon, diced
1/3 cup boiling water	1/2 cup all-purpose flour
1 package (16 ounces)	4 cups milk
Frozen Stokely's®	Pepper to taste
Size Wize® Vegetables	
Sized for Soup	

Add salt to water and cook vegetables until tender, about 5 minutes. Cook bacon in 2-quart saucepan over low heat, stirring frequently. Measure drippings, reserving 1/2 cup in pan. Add flour to drippings and mix well. Stir in milk and cook, stirring constantly, until thickened. Season with pepper. Add vegetables and heat through.   *4 to 6 servings*

HOME-STYLE VEGETABLE SOUP

Effortless and nourishing.

1 teaspoon salt	1/2 cup Stokely's Finest®
1 bay leaf	Tomato Catsup
1 dash pepper	4 cups water
1 can (10 3/4 ounces)	1 package (16 ounces)
beef broth	Frozen Stokely's®
1 Tablespoon instant	Size Wize® Vegetables
beef flavored	Sized for Soup
bouillon	

Place all ingredients except vegetables in 4-quart saucepan and heat to boiling. Add vegetables and return to boil. Reduce heat, cover, and simmer 30 minutes.   *4 to 6 servings*

BUTTER BEAN SOUP

Fast and excellent.

1 can (15 ounces)
Van Camp's®
Butter Beans
1 can (16 ounces)
Stokely's Finest®
Stewed Tomatoes
3 Tablespoons butter or
margarine

1 Tablespoon instant
minced onion
1 1/2 teaspoons sugar
1/4 teaspoon seasoned salt
Dash pepper

Combine all ingredients in saucepan, cover, and simmer 30 minutes. *3 to 4 servings*

Microwave Method: Combine all ingredients in 2-quart casserole. Cover and microcook 6 minutes, or until heated through. Stir twice.

QUICK CHILEE WEENEE TACOS

The spicy chili flavor and ease of preparation make these tacos ideal for teen-age parties.

2 cans (7 3/4 ounces each)
Van Camp's® Chilee
Weenee®
6 taco shells

1 cup shredded lettuce
3/4 cup shredded Cheddar
cheese
Chopped tomato

Heat chilee weenee to serving temperature and warm taco shells a few minutes in 300°F. oven. Arrange lettuce in taco shells; spoon on chilee weenee. Sprinkle with cheese and chopped tomato. Serve immediately. *6 tacos*

Variation:

Substitute 3 English muffins, split and toasted, for the taco shells.

Opposite: Butter Bean Soup, Quick Chilee Weenee Tacos

ICED SWEET CHERRY SOUP

Try this refreshingly different recipe.

2 packages (16 ounces
    each) Frozen Stokely's®
    Dark Sweet Cherries
1 cup sugar
1 teaspoon cinnamon
2 1/2 cups water
1 lemon

2 Tablespoons cornstarch
1 cup dry white wine
  Sprigs of fresh mint
    (optional)
  Commercial sour cream
    (optional)

Place cherries, sugar, and cinnamon in medium-size saucepan. Add water. Grate 1 teaspoon rind from lemon and add to saucepan; squeeze 2 Tablespoons juice and add to saucepan. Bring mixture to boil over medium heat, cover, lower heat, and simmer 10 to 12 minutes. Meanwhile place cornstarch in small bowl and add small amount of wine; stir to form smooth paste. Add remaining wine and stir. Pour into saucepan and stir until mixture reaches boiling point and thickens. Lower heat and simmer, uncovered, 5 minutes. Remove from heat and pour into blender or food processor; purée. Allow soup to cool; refrigerate several hours. Serve ice cold in small bowls. Garnish with sprigs of fresh mint or dollop of sour cream.   *4 to 6 servings*

SOUP-ERB BROCCOLI AND HAM

Delightful for Sunday night supper.

2 Tablespoons butter or
    margarine
3/4 cup sliced mushrooms
1 can (11 ounces)
    condensed Cheddar
    cheese soup,
    undiluted
1 1/2 cups cubed cooked ham

1 box (10 ounces)
    Frozen Stokely's®
    Chopped Broccoli,
    cooked (omitting
    salt) and drained
4 hard-cooked eggs,
    sliced
3 English muffins, split

Melt butter in medium-size saucepan. Add mushrooms and sauté about 3 minutes. Stir in soup, ham, and broccoli. Cook over moderate heat about 5 minutes. Gently fold in all but 6 egg slices. Spoon over toasted muffin halves. Garnish each serving with egg slice.   *6 servings*

NUTTY BROCCOLI SALAD

Raw broccoli adds crunchy goodness to this salad.

1 package (10 ounces)
Frozen Stokely's®
Chopped Broccoli,
thawed
2 cups diced cooked
chicken
1/4 cup chopped dry roasted
cashews

2 teaspoons lemon juice
3/4 cup mayonnaise
1/4 cup Russian dressing
6 lettuce leaves
1 jar (2 ounces)
Stokely's Finest®
Sliced Pimientos,
drained

Thoroughly drain broccoli and place in medium-size bowl. Add chicken, cashews, lemon juice, mayonnaise, and Russian dressing to bowl and combine well. Spoon chicken mixture over lettuce and garnish with sliced pimientos.   *6 servings*

MID-EAST CURRIED PORK SANDWICHES

An after-the-ballgame treat!

1 large onion, chopped
2 cloves garlic, minced
2 Tablespoons vegetable oil
2 pounds lean ground
pork
3/4 teaspoon ginger
3/4 teaspoon curry powder
2 Tablespoons soy sauce
2/3 cup sweet pickle relish
1 to 2 Tablespoons hot
pepper sauce (or to
taste)

1 can (16 ounces)
Van Camp's® Pork
and Beans
1 1/2 teaspoons sugar
1 teaspoon cider vinegar
3/4 cup plain yogurt
10 pita breads
Tomato slices
Chopped scallions
(green onions)

Sauté onion and garlic in hot oil until onion is transparent. Add pork and cook about 20 minutes over low heat, stirring occasionally, until pink color disappears and meat is lightly browned. Drain excess fat. Add ginger, curry, soy sauce, relish, pepper sauce, pork and beans, sugar, and vinegar; blend gently and continue cooking over low heat 10 minutes. Add yogurt, stir and heat to just under boiling. Split pita breads in half crosswise. Carefully fill pockets with meat mixture. Garnish by placing half slice of tomato wedged into opening and sprinkle with chopped scallions.   *10 servings*

FLORENTINE SUBMARINES

Perfect for a light snack — good nutrition and great flavors!

1 package (16 ounces)
   Frozen Stokely's®
   Broccoli Florentine®
1 loaf of French bread or
   4 garlic bagels
   Garlic powder

Grated mozzarella
   cheese
1/2 cup commercial sour
   cream
1/2 cup mayonnaise

Cook broccoli according to package directions; drain and blot with paper towels. Split and quarter bread and sprinkle with garlic powder. Divide cooked broccoli into 4 portions and place each portion on a bread quarter or split bagel. Top with grated cheese. Broil until cheese is slightly brown and bubbly. Meanwhile, combine sour cream and mayonnaise and mix well. Remove sandwiches from broiler and top each with a dollop of sour cream sauce. Serve immediately.   *4 to 6 servings*

REUBEN SANDWICHES

Try it . . . you'll love it!

16 slices rye bread
 8 slices Swiss Cheese
 1 pound thinly sliced
   corned beef
 1 can (16 ounces)
   Stokely's Finest®
   Bavarian Style
   Sauerkraut, drained

1/2 cup Thousand Island
   dressing
 2 eggs, lightly beaten
1/3 cup milk
1/2 teaspoon sugar
   Dash salt
 3 Tablespoons butter or
   margarine, melted

On 8 slices of bread, place Swiss cheese, corned beef, sauerkraut, and 1 Tablespoon dressing; top with second bread slice. Combine eggs, milk, sugar, and salt in shallow dish. Melt butter in skillet. Dip both sides of sandwich in egg mixture and brown each side in skillet until golden.   *8 sandwiches*

Opposite: Stokely's Finest® Orange Juice, Florentine Submarine, Reuben Sandwich

BARBECUED BEEF

Great way to use leftover roast beef.

1 Tablespoon butter or
   margarine
1/2 cup chopped onion
1 can (8 ounces)
   Stokely's Finest®
   Tomato Sauce
1/4 cup firmly packed
   brown sugar
3 Tablespoons lemon juice
3 Tablespoons
   Stokely's Finest®
   Tomato Catsup

1 Tablespoon
   Worcestershire sauce
1 teaspoon salt
1 teaspoon dry mustard
1/8 teaspoon garlic powder
3 cups diced cooked
   roast beef

Melt butter in large skillet; sauté onion in butter until transparent. Stir in remaining ingredients except beef and heat until bubbling. Add beef, cover, and simmer 30 minutes, stirring occasionally. Serve on buns. *8 servings*

Microwave Method: Place butter in 2-quart casserole and microcook 30 seconds. Add onion and microcook 1 to 2 minutes, or until onion is tender, stirring once. Add remaining ingredients, except beef, cover, and microcook 3 minutes, or until bubbling. Add beef, cover, and microcook 3 additional minutes, stirring once.

HOT TUNA SANDWICHES

Kids can make their own.

1 can (6 1/2 ounces)
   tuna, drained and
   flaked
2 Tablespoons mayonnaise
1 Tablespoon chopped
   celery
1 Tablespoon chopped
   onion

1/8 teaspoon salt
1 can (8 1/2 ounces)
   Stokely's Finest® Peas,
   drained
4 slices bread, toasted
4 slices Swiss cheese

Combine tuna, mayonnaise, celery, onion, and salt. Carefully fold in peas; spread mixture on toast. Broil 3 minutes; top each sandwich with cheese and broil until cheese begins to melt.
4 open-faced sandwiches

CRÊPE SANDWICH TORTE

Delicious, different, and bound to cause "table talk."

8 8-inch crêpes
   Mayonnaise (optional)
   Prepared mustard
   (optional)
1/4 pound thinly sliced
   ham
1/4 pound thinly sliced
   Swiss cheese

1 package (10 ounces)
   Frozen Stokely's®
   Leaf Spinach, cooked,
   drained, and cooled
1 cup egg salad

Sour Cream-Mustard Sauce

1/2 cup white sauce
1/4 cup commercial sour
   cream

1/2 teaspoon prepared
   mustard
   Salt and pepper to taste

To build an 8-tier sandwich, place 1 crêpe on a plate for the bottom layer. As you build the sandwich, spread each crêpe with mayonnaise or mustard according to your taste. Top first crêpe with half the ham and another crêpe; add half the cheese and another crêpe; add half the spinach and another crêpe, then half the egg salad. Repeat layers. Refrigerate 30 minutes before serving. To serve, cut sandwich into wedges and serve with warm Sour Cream-Mustard Sauce, if desired.   *4 servings*

Sour Cream-Mustard Sauce
To make sauce, mix all sauce ingredients together, warm, and serve over sandwich wedges.

JIFFY LUNCH

A three-minute meal.

1 can (7 3/4 ounces)
Van Camp's® Beanee
Weenee®
2 teaspoons chopped onion

1 Tablespoon
Stokely's Finest®
Tomato Catsup
Corn chips

Heat beanee weenee, onion, and catsup together until warmed through. Place in serving dish and crumble corn chips over top. *1 serving*

A SKETTEE WEENEE MEAL

Heat, eat, and enjoy! Ideal for all ages.

1 can (7 3/4 ounces)
Van Camp's® Skettee
Weenee

Tossed salad
1 apple

In a saucepan or microwave oven, heat skettee weenee to serving temperature. Serve with a tossed green salad and a juicy apple for dessert. *1 serving*

NOODLEE WEENEE SURPRISES

Youngsters will love this special lunch treat.

2 cans (7 3/4 ounces each)
Van Camp's® Noodlee
Weenee
2 Tablespoons chopped
onion (optional)

2 Tablespoons chopped
green pepper
(optional)
1/2 cup shredded mozzarella
cheese

Preheat oven to 350°. Place noodlee weenee in individual casseroles. Top each with chopped onion and green pepper. Sprinkle with cheese and bake 15 minutes, or until noodles are warm and cheese is melted. Serve immediately. *4 servings*

Main Dishes

SWEDISH CABBAGE ROLLS

A Scandinavian specialty.

6 large cabbage leaves	1/2 cup cubed pasteurized process cheese spread
1/2 pound lean ground beef	1 egg, beaten
1/2 cup cooked rice	1/4 teaspoon salt
1 can (8 1/2 ounces) Stokely's Finest® Whole Kernel Golden Corn, drained, liquid reserved	Dash pepper
	1/2 teaspoon Worcestershire sauce
2 Tablespoons finely chopped onion	1 can (8 ounces) Stokely's Finest® Tomato Sauce

Steam cabbage leaves 3 minutes in covered pan; drain and set aside. Brown ground beef in skillet; drain excess fat. Add rice, corn, onion, cheese, egg, salt, pepper, and Worcestershire sauce to meat in skillet. Place 1/2 cup meat mixture on each reserved cabbage leaf. Fold in sides and roll up ends; secure with toothpick.

Place rolls, folded side up, in 10-inch skillet. Combine tomato sauce and reserved corn liquid. Pour over cabbage rolls, cover, and simmer 30 minutes.   *6 servings*

MEXICAN PIE

A pretty dish with little effort.

1 1/4 cups biscuit mix	1 can (15 1/2 ounces)
1/4 cup commercial sour	Van Camp's® Mexican
cream	Style Chili Beans
1 egg, beaten	1/2 cup shredded lettuce
1 pound lean ground beef	1 cup diced fresh tomato
1 teaspoon salt	3/4 cup grated Monterey
1/2 cup chopped onion	Jack cheese

Preheat oven to 425°F. Combine biscuit mix, sour cream, and egg. Mix to form soft dough. With lightly floured hands, spread dough on bottom and up sides of greased 10×6×1 3/4-inch pan. Brown ground beef; drain excess fat. Add salt, onion, and chili beans; mix well and spoon into crust. Bake 20 to 30 minutes, or until edge of crust is deep golden brown. Top with lettuce, tomato, and cheese. Let stand 5 minutes before cutting.   *6 servings*

BISCUIT-TOPPED BEEF 'N BEANS

An easy way to top a casserole.

1 pound lean ground beef	1 can (15 ounces)
3 Tablespoons chopped	Van Camp's® New
onion	Orleans Style Red
3 Tablespoons chopped	Kidney Beans
green pepper	1 can (7 1/2 ounces)
1 teaspoon seasoned salt	refrigerated light
1 Tablespoon	buttermilk biscuits
Worcestershire sauce	(10 biscuits)
1/2 cup Stokely's Finest®	1 Tablespoon butter or
Tomato Catsup	margarine, melted
2 Tablespoons brown sugar	1/4 cup grated Parmesan
2 teaspoons cider vinegar	cheese

Preheat oven to 425°F. In large skillet, brown ground beef, onion, and green pepper; drain excess fat. Blend in remaining ingredients except biscuits, butter, and Parmesan cheese. Heat thoroughly in skillet. Spoon mixture into 1 1/2-quart casserole. Top with biscuits; brush biscuit tops with butter and sprinkle with cheese. Bake 10 to 12 minutes, or until biscuits are browned on top.   *5 to 6 servings*

FIESTA MEATBALL SUPPER

A colorful mouth-watering dish.

1 egg, beaten
1/2 cup finely chopped onion
1 cup soft bread crumbs
3/4 teaspoon salt
1/8 teaspoon garlic powder
1/8 teaspoon pepper
1 pound ground beef
1 Tablespoon vegetable shortening
1 can (16 ounces) Stokely's Finest® Stewed Tomatoes
1 can (15 ounces) Van Camp's® Red Beans
1 can (12 ounces) Stokely's Finest® Vacuum Packed Whole Kernel Golden Corn
1 can (8 ounces) Stokely's Finest® Tomato Sauce
1 1/2 teaspoons chili powder
1 bay leaf
1 cup shredded mild Cheddar cheese
1 cup crushed corn chips

In large bowl combine egg, onion, bread crumbs, salt, garlic powder, and pepper until mixed. Add ground beef and mix well. With wet hands shape meat mixture into twenty-four 1-inch meatballs. In large skillet add shortening, place skillet over medium heat, and brown meatballs on all sides. Remove excess drippings. In large bowl combine tomatoes, beans, corn, tomato sauce, and chili powder. Pour mixture over meatballs in skillet. Add bay leaf. Bring to a boil, then reduce heat and simmer for 30 minutes, covered. Remove bay leaf. Serve with shredded cheese and chips. *6 servings*

Microwave Method: In a large bowl combine egg, onion, bread crumbs, salt, garlic powder, and pepper until mixed. Add ground beef and mix well. With wet hands shape meat mixture into twenty-four 1-inch meatballs. Place meatballs in 12×7×2-inch baking dish. Omit shortening in this method. Microcook, covered, until done, about 6 minutes, turning meatballs twice. Drain off excess fat.

In another large bowl combine tomatoes, beans, corn, tomato sauce, and chili powder. Pour mixture over meatballs. Add bay leaf. Microcook, covered, for 12 minutes, stirring every 4 minutes. Remove bay leaf. Serve with shredded cheese and chips.

BEEF STEW THREE WAYS

No matter which cooking method you choose, this recipe is always a favorite.

2 Tablespoons vegetable
shortening
1 1/2 pounds beef for
stewing, cut into
1 1/2-inch cubes
Salt and pepper to taste
1 cup beef broth
1 can (16 ounces)
Stokely's Finest®
Stewed Tomatoes
1 bay leaf

1/2 teaspoon garlic powder
1/2 teaspoon sugar
1/4 teaspoon thyme
1 package (20 ounces)
Frozen Stokely's®
Size Wize® Vegetables
Sized for Stew
2 Tablespoons
Stokely's Finest®
Tomato Catsup

Melt shortening in large heavy saucepan or Dutch oven. Brown meat on all sides; season with salt and pepper. Add broth, tomatoes, bay leaf, garlic powder, sugar, and thyme. Stir well, cover, and simmer 2 hours. Add vegetables and simmer, covered, an additional 30 minutes, or until meat and vegetables are fork tender. Remove bay leaf, stir in catsup, adjust seasoning, and cook 5 minutes longer.   *6 servings*

Slow Cook Method: Melt shortening in large skillet. Brown meat on all sides; season with salt and pepper. Transfer to slow cooker, add broth, tomatoes, bay leaf, garlic powder, sugar, and thyme, and vegetables. Stir to mix, cover and cook on low 6 to 8 hours, or high 3 to 4 hours. Remove bay leaf, stir in catsup, adjust seasoning, cook on high 10 minutes longer.

Pressure Cooker Method: Remove trivet from pressure cooker and melt shortening. Brown meat on all sides; season with salt and pepper. Add broth, tomatoes, bay leaf, garlic powder, sugar, and thyme. Stir well, cover, and cook 8 minutes at 15 pounds pressure. Cool quickly. Add vegetables, cover, and cook 3 minutes at 15 pounds pressure. Cool quickly; remove bay leaf, stir in catsup, adjust seasoning, and cook, uncovered, 5 minutes longer.

CORN O'PLENTY

From a Tennessee recipe contest.

2 Tablespoons butter or margarine
1 jar or package (about 3 ounces) dried beef, shredded
2 Tablespoons finely chopped onion
1 Tablespoon all-purpose flour
3/4 cup milk
1 can (17 ounces) Stokely's Finest® Cream Style Golden Corn
1/2 cup shredded sharp Cheddar cheese
2 Tablespoons finely chopped green pepper
Toast cups

Melt butter in skillet and sauté beef and onion until beef begins to curl; remove from heat and blend in flour. Stir in milk and cook over medium heat until thickened. Add corn and heat through. Stir in cheese and green pepper. Heat until cheese melts. Serve in toast cups or over toast.   *4 to 5 servings*

To make toast cups:

Preheat oven to 375°F. Remove crusts from 8 to 10 slices thin sandwich bread. Spread bread on both sides with softened butter. Press each slice into muffin tin and bake 12 minutes.

SKILLET GOULASH

An excellent way to stretch ground beef.

1/2 pound lean ground beef
1/4 cup chopped onion
1 can (16 ounces) Stokely's Finest® Stewed Tomatoes
1 can (15 ounces) Van Camp's® New Orleans Style Red Kidney Beans
1/2 cup macaroni
1 teaspoon salt
1 teaspoon sugar
1/2 teaspoon chili powder
1/4 teaspoon cumin
Dash pepper

Brown ground beef and onion in large skillet; drain excess fat. Add remaining ingredients and simmer, covered, 30 to 40 minutes, stirring occasionally, or until macaroni is cooked and tender.
4 servings

TEXAS CHILI

A "real" chili that is economical, delicious, and easy to make.

1/2 pound lean ground beef
1/2 cup chopped onion
1/2 cup chopped green
   pepper
1/4 cup chopped celery
  1 package (1 1/4 ounces)
   chili seasoning mix
  1 can (8 ounces)
   Stokely's Finest®
   Tomato Sauce

1 can (15 ounces)
   Stokely's Finest®
   Dark Red Kidney Beans
For garnish: chopped
   onion, chopped green
   pepper, grated cheese,
   or commercial sour
   cream

Place beef, onion, green pepper, and celery in large skillet. Cook over medium heat, stirring constantly, until meat is browned and vegetables are tender. Drain excess fat. Stir in remaining ingredients, cover, and simmer 30 minutes. Top with chopped onion, chopped green pepper, grated cheese, or sour cream.   *4 servings*

Microwave Method: Crumble beef in 1 1/2-quart casserole. Add onion, green pepper, and celery. Microcook, covered, 6 minutes, stirring twice. Drain excess fat. Stir in remaining ingredients, cover, and microcook 5 minutes, stirring once. Top with chopped onion, chopped green pepper, grated cheese, or sour cream.

Opposite: Mexican Corn Bread (page 143), Texas Chili

SOMBRERO PIE

A hearty tasty meal.

1 pound lean ground beef	1 1/2 Tablespoons chili powder
1 medium-size onion, sliced	1 teaspoon salt
1/2 cup Stokely's Finest® Tomato Juice	1/4 teaspoon pepper
1 package (16 ounces) Frozen Stokely's® Chuckwagon Corn	

Pastry:

1 1/4 cups all-purpose flour	1/2 cup vegetable oil
1/2 cup cornmeal	3 Tablespoons cold water
1 teaspoon salt	

Sauté beef and onion in a large skillet until onion is transparent and meat is browned. Drain excess fat. Stir in remaining ingredients and simmer 10 minutes. Pour into 11×7×1-inch baking dish and set aside. Preheat oven to 400°F. To make pastry, mix flour, cornmeal, and salt. Make a well in center of mixture and add oil. Stir until mixture resembles fine crumbs. Sprinkle water, a Tablespoon at a time, over mixture, and stir with fork until mixture forms ball. If too dry, work in 1 or 2 Tablespoons additional oil. Roll pastry between 2 sheets of waxed paper, making a 12×8-inch rectangle. Peel off top paper and invert pastry onto filled baking dish. Peel off second piece of waxed paper and cut 3 or 4 slits in pastry to make a sombrero design on top. Bake 30 to 35 minutes.   *4 to 6 servings*

SPANISH STUFFED PEPPERS

Spanish rice makes this recipe quick to fix.

3 green bell peppers	2 Tablespoons Stokely's Finest® Tomato Catsup
1 pound lean ground beef	
3 Tablespoons chopped onion	Parmesan cheese
1 can (15 ounces) Van Camp's® Spanish Rice	

Preheat oven to 350°F. Cut peppers in half lengthwise; discard seeds and pith. Steam 5 minutes in covered pan with 1 inch of water; cool quickly. Meanwhile, brown ground beef and onion in skillet; drain excess fat. Stir in Spanish rice and catsup. Spoon beef mixture into pepper halves. Place filled peppers upright in 12×8-inch baking dish. Bake 25 to 30 minutes. Sprinkle with Parmesan cheese and serve immediately.   *6 pepper halves*

Microwave Method: Cut peppers in half lengthwise; discard seeds and pith. Place, cut side up, in 12×8-inch baking dish. Cover with waxed paper and microcook 7 minutes, turning dish once; set aside. Crumble ground beef in 1 1/2-quart casserole; stir in onion. Microcook, covered, 4 minutes, stirring once; drain excess fat. Stir in Spanish rice and catsup. Spoon beef mixture into pepper halves. Cover with waxed paper and microcook 12 minutes, turning dish twice. Sprinkle with Parmesan cheese and serve immediately.

TEXAS-STYLE BEEF AND BEANS

Just add a crisp salad and hot cornbread for a complete meal.

1 **pound lean ground beef**	3 **Tablespoons vegetable oil**
1 **small onion, finely chopped**	2 **packages (10 ounces each) Frozen Stokely's® Baby Lima Beans**
2 **eggs, beaten**	
1/2 **cup seasoned bread crumbs**	1 **cup bottled hickory smoke-flavored barbecue sauce**
Salt and pepper to taste	
1 **clove garlic, minced**	**Hot pepper sauce**
2 **teaspoons chili powder**	1/4 **cup water**
3/4 **cup Stokely's Finest® Tomato Catsup, divided**	

Combine beef, onion, eggs, bread crumbs, salt, pepper, garlic, chili powder, and 1/4 cup catsup in medium-size bowl and mix well. Shape into 24 balls, about 1-inch in diameter. Heat oil in large skillet and brown meatballs well on all sides. Drain and discard excess fat from skillet. Add beans, barbecue sauce, hot pepper sauce, remaining 1/2 cup catsup, and water to skillet; stir and bring to a boil. Lower heat, cover, and simmer 15 to 20 minutes, or until beans are tender.   *4 to 6 servings*

CHUCKWAGON PEPPER STEAK

Serve with rice for a complete meal.

1 1/2 pounds top round steak
3 Tablespoons vegetable
   shortening
1 medium-size onion,
   chopped
1 clove garlic, minced
1 can (16 ounces)
   Stokely's Finest®
   Stewed Tomatoes, chopped

1/2 cup beef broth
2 Tablespoons soy sauce
1 1/2 Tablespoons cornstarch
1/2 of 16-ounce package
   (8 ounces)
   Frozen Stokely's®
   Chuckwagon Corn

Thinly slice steak against the grain. Melt shortening in large skillet over high heat, add meat, and brown quickly. Lower heat, add onion and garlic, and cook until onion is transparent. Add tomatoes and beef broth to skillet; stir to combine. Bring to a boil, lower heat, cover, and simmer 20 minutes. Combine soy sauce and cornstarch and add to skillet, stirring until mixture is slightly thickened. Add corn and simmer 5 to 6 minutes longer, stirring occasionally.
6 servings

SWISS STEAK AND VEGETABLES

A mouth-watering treat.

3 Tablespoons all-purpose
   flour
1/2 teaspoon salt
1/8 teaspoon pepper
1 1/2- to 2-pound beef chuck
   arm steak
2 Tablespoons vegetable
   oil
1 can (16 ounces)
   Stokely's Finest®
   Stewed Tomatoes

3/4 cup beef broth or water
1 package (28 ounces)
   Frozen Stokely's®
   Size Wize® Vegetables
   Sized for Roast
1 can (4 1/2 ounces) sliced
   mushrooms, drained

Combine flour, salt, and pepper. Dust meat on both sides with flour mixture. Heat oil in Dutch oven and brown meat on both sides. Combine tomatoes and broth and pour over meat. Bring to a boil, lower heat, cover, and simmer 45 minutes. Add vegetables and mushrooms. Cook, covered, an additional 45 minutes, or until vegetables are tender. *4 servings*

CRUNCHY BEEF AND SHELLIE BEANS

Serve over hot cooked noodles.

1 pound flank steak
2 Tablespoons vegetable oil
1 large onion, thinly sliced
1 clove garlic, minced
1 cup beef broth
1 can (16 ounces) Stokely's Finest® Shellie® Beans, drained
1 teaspoon tarragon
1 can (8 ounces) water chestnuts, drained and sliced
1/4 cup dry red wine
3 Tablespoons soy sauce
2 Tablespoons cornstarch
Hot cooked noodles

Thinly slice meat across the grain. Heat oil in large skillet. Add sliced beef and brown quickly over high heat. Lower heat, add onion and garlic, and cook until onion is transparent. Add broth, beans, tarragon, and water chestnuts; cook 2 minutes. Meanwhile, combine wine, soy sauce, and cornstarch. Gradually stir cornstarch mixture into skillet and cook until thickened, about 2 to 3 minutes. Remove from heat and serve over noodles.   *4 servings*

SMOTHERED STEAKS

Serve with a vegetable and you have a meal.

4 cube steaks
About 1/2 cup all-purpose flour
1/4 cup vegetable oil
Seasoned salt
Pepper
1 medium-size onion, sliced
1 can (15 ounces) Van Camp's® Spanish Rice
1 teaspoon sugar
1 teaspoon parsley flakes

Preheat oven to 325°F. Coat steaks with flour. In skillet, brown steaks in oil and transfer to greased 9-inch square baking dish. Sprinkle with seasoned salt and pepper and set aside. Sauté onion slices in skillet drippings; add Spanish rice and sugar; mix well. Spoon rice mixture over steaks and sprinkle with parsley flakes. Bake, uncovered, 30 minutes.   *4 servings*

COLONIAL POT ROAST

A "no-watch" meal.

2 Tablespoons vegetable
oil
1 3-pound boneless beef
chuck roast
Salt and pepper
1 can (16 ounces)
Stokely's Finest®
Stewed Tomatoes

1 teaspoon sugar
1 teaspoon oregano
1 package (28 ounces)
Frozen Stokely's®
Size Wize® Vegetables
Sized for Roast
All-purpose flour
(optional)

Heat oil in Dutch oven. Season meat with salt and pepper and brown on all sides over medium heat, about 15 minutes. Add tomatoes, sugar, and oregano. Cover and simmer 2 1/2 to 3 hours. Add vegetables and continue cooking, covered, 1 hour, or until meat and vegetables are tender. Lift meat and vegetables from pan with slotted spoon. If gravy is desired, measure sauce from Dutch oven. Add 2 Tablespoons flour to each cup of drippings; blend and return to Dutch oven. Heat, stirring constantly, until thickened. Adjust seasoning. Serve with meat and vegetables.   *4 to 6 servings*

BEEF IN A PACKET

A cooking method that eliminates pot watching.

1 4-pound boneless,
rolled, bottom round
rump roast
1 package (28 ounces)
Frozen Stokely's® Size
Wize® Vegetables Sized
for Roast

1 envelope (1 1/3 ounces)
onion soup mix
1/4 cup water

Preheat oven to 350°F. Place roast in Dutch oven or in center of large piece of aluminum foil. Surround meat with vegetables, sprinkle with soup mix, and pour water over all. Cover Dutch oven or wrap meat securely with foil and place in roasting pan. Bake until meat thermometer registers 150°F to 170°F, approximately 2 hours. Let meat stand about 15 minutes before carving.   *6 servings*

Opposite: Colonial Pot Roast

PRESSURE COOKER ROAST

Energy saving and tasty.

1 can (16 ounces)
  Stokely's Finest®
  Stewed Tomatoes
2 Tablespoons instant
  minced onion

2 teaspoons instant beef
  bouillon
1/2 cup water
1 3-pound beef chuck
  roast

Combine tomatoes, onion, bouillon, and water in 4- to 6-quart pressure cooker. Add roast. Cover and set control at 10 pounds pressure. After pressure is reached, cook 50 minutes. Remove pressure cooker from heat and let stand 5 minutes; place under cool running water to reduce pressure completely. Remove meat to platter. Spoon sauce over meat as is or thicken slightly with flour for gravy.   *6 servings*

Nice to know: Meat may be browned in open pressure cooker before adding other ingredients.

CORNY BEEF CASSEROLE

A quick one-dish meal.

1 pound lean ground beef
1/2 cup finely chopped
  green pepper
1/2 cup chopped onion
1 can (15 ounces)
  Stokely's Finest®
  Dark Red Kidney Beans
1 can (8 ounces)
  Stokely's Finest®
  Tomato Sauce

1/2 cup sliced black olives
1/2 teaspoon salt
1/4 teaspoon garlic powder
1 package (8 1/2 ounces)
  corn muffin mix
1/2 cup shredded Cheddar
  cheese

Preheat oven to 375°F. In skillet, brown ground beef, green pepper, and onion; drain excess fat. Stir in kidney beans, tomato sauce, olives, salt, and garlic powder; spread into a greased 9-inch square pan. Prepare muffin mix according to package directions; stir in cheese and spread batter over beef mixture. Bake 30 to 35 minutes.   *6 servings*

SLOW-COOKED BOILED DINNER

Just turn on the slow cooker before you leave in the morning and presto, when you return home — dinner is almost ready.

1 3-pound corned beef brisket	Pepper to taste
1 bay leaf	1 medium-size head cabbage, cut into wedges
1 package (28 ounces) Frozen Stokely's® Size Wize® Vegetables Sized for Roast	

Place meat in bottom of 6-quart slow cooker. Add bay leaf. Lay frozen vegetables on top of meat, and sprinkle with pepper. Pour in enough water to barely cover vegetables. Add cabbage, cover, and cook 8 to 10 hours on low, 4 to 6 hours on high. Remove bay leaf, drain, and serve.   *6 servings*

BEEF CHOP SUEY

Serve when your family wants something unusual.

1 pound top round steak	1 can (16 ounces) bean sprouts
3 Tablespoons soy sauce	
2 Tablespoons vegetable oil	1 1/2 Tablespoons cornstarch Chow mein noodles
1 cup chopped celery	
1/2 cup water	
1 package (16 ounces) Frozen Stokely's® Vegetables Orient®	

Thinly slice steak against the grain, place in shallow dish; pour soy sauce over, stir to coat, and let marinate 15 to 20 minutes. Heat oil in large skillet, add celery and sauté 3 minutes over high heat. Push celery to one side of skillet, drain steak, reserving soy sauce, and add steak to skillet. Brown quickly on both sides. Add water and frozen vegetables, lower heat, cover, and cook 5 minutes. Meanwhile drain bean sprouts into colander and rinse under very cold running water 1 minute to crisp. Combine cornstarch with reserved soy sauce and add to skillet, stirring constantly, until mixture is slightly thickened. Add bean sprouts to skillet and cook 2 minutes, stirring occasionally. Serve over chow mein noodles.   *6 to 8 servings*

CANTONESE FLANK STEAK

For an interesting variation, substitute shrimp for beef (or use half beef, half shrimp).

1/2 pound flank steak	1 teaspoon plus 1
2 Tablespoons cornstarch	Tablespoon vegetable
1 teaspoon sugar	oil, divided
1/2 teaspoon ginger	1 package (14 ounces)
1/2 cup dry sherry	Frozen Stokely's®
2 Tablespoons soy sauce	Cantonese Style Stir
1/3 cup water	Fry Vegetables

Cut flank steak across the grain into paper-thin strips. Place in glass dish. Blend cornstarch, sugar, ginger, sherry, soy sauce, and water to make marinade. Pour marinade over meat. Refrigerate, covered, 2 1/2 hours. Remove meat from marinade and drain, reserving marinade. Heat 9- or 10-inch skillet or wok over high heat (a drop of water will sizzle). Pour 1 teaspoon oil in wide, circular motion inside rim of pan. Tilt pan to coat surface. Add half the meat and stir-fry about 3 minutes. Remove to warm serving dish. Cook remaining meat about 3 minutes and remove to serving dish. Remove seasoning packet from vegetables and reserve. When skillet is again very hot, spread frozen vegetables evenly in pan. Pour 1 Tablespoon oil in pan in circular motion and stir into vegetables quickly, coating each piece. Sprinkle reserved seasoning packet over vegetables and add 2 Tablespoons water and reserved marinade in circular motion. Cook and stir about 30 seconds until vegetables and seasonings are blended. Cover and cook 1 minute, return meat to skillet, stir, and cook 1 minute more. Serve immediately.
4 servings

Note: For easier slicing, partially freeze flank steak.

Opposite: Cantonese Flank Steak, Chinese Chicken with Cherries (page 84)

MOZZARELLA MEAT LOAF

If you fix it, your family will love it!

1 1/2 pounds lean ground beef
1/2 cup dry bread crumbs
1 egg, slightly beaten
1 teaspoon instant minced onion
3/4 teaspoon salt
1/2 teaspoon oregano

1 can (15 ounces) Stokely's Finest® Tomato Sauce, divided
1 1/2 cups shredded mozzarella cheese
1 can (4 ounces) mushroom stems and pieces, drained, (optional)

Preheat oven to 375°F. Grease 12×8×2-inch baking pan. In mixing bowl combine ground beef, bread crumbs, egg, onion, salt, and oregano. Stir in 3/4 cup tomato sauce. Cut a piece of waxed paper 15 inches long. Press meat into a 13×9-inch rectangle on waxed paper. Sprinkle meat with cheese, top with mushrooms. Starting with narrow end of meat, lift waxed paper to help roll meat jelly-roll fashion. Place meat seam side down in prepared pan. Bake 30 minutes. Remove excess drippings from baking pan. Pour remaining tomato sauce over meat loaf. Bake an additional 30 minutes.
8 servings

BEEF PARMIGIANA

A traditional Italian dish.

1 1/2 pounds top round steak, cut about 1/2-inch thick
1/3 cup dry bread crumbs
1/3 cup grated Parmesan cheese
1 egg, beaten
1/3 cup vegetable oil
1 large onion, chopped
1 can (16 ounces) Stokely's Finest® Stewed Tomatoes

1 can (8 ounces) Stokely's Finest® Tomato Sauce
Salt and pepper to taste
1 teaspoon basil
1/2 teaspoon oregano
1 1/2 cups grated mozzarella cheese

Trim excess fat from steak; cut into 6 pieces; pound each piece with heavy mallet to about 1/4-inch thickness. Combine bread crumbs and Parmesan cheese. Dip each piece of meat in beaten egg, then in crumb mixture. Heat oil in large skillet and brown steak well on both sides. Remove steak to paper towels to drain. Add onion, stewed tomatoes, tomato sauce, salt, pepper, basil, and oregano to skillet and stir to combine. Bring mixture to a boil, lower heat, and simmer, uncovered, 30 minutes. Meanwhile, preheat oven to 350°F. Spoon 5 Tablespoons cooked tomato mixture into bottom of 9×13×2-inch baking dish (enough to lightly cover bottom of dish). Place steak on top of sauce in single layer. Pour remaining sauce over steak and bake 1 hour. Remove from oven and sprinkle with cheese. Bake an additional 15 minutes, or until cheese is melted.   *6 servings*

Helpful hint: When food is baked in a glass dish, oven temperature should be reduced by 25°F.

LASAGNA

May be refrigerated and baked later.

1 1/2 **pounds lean ground beef**	1/4 **teaspoon oregano**
1/2 **cup chopped onion**	1/8 **teaspoon pepper**
1/2 **cup chopped green pepper**	8 **ounces lasagna noodles,**
1 **can (16 ounces)**	**uncooked**
Stokely's Finest®	2 **cups cottage cheese**
Tomatoes, cut up	2 **eggs, beaten**
2 **cans (8 ounces each)**	1 **can (8 ounces)**
Stokely's Finest®	**Stokely's Finest®**
Tomato Sauce	**Spinach, well drained**
1/2 **cup Stokely's Finest®**	**and chopped (optional)**
Tomato Catsup	1/2 **teaspoon salt**
2 **Tablespoons minced**	3 **cups shredded**
parsley	**mozzarella cheese**
1 1/2 **teaspoons salt**	**(12 ounces)**
1 **teaspoon basil**	1/2 **cup grated Parmesan**
1/4 **teaspoon garlic powder**	**cheese**

Preheat oven to 350°F. Grease a 13×9×2-inch casserole. Brown beef, onion, and green pepper in skillet. Drain excess fat. Add tomatoes, tomato sauce, catsup, parsley, salt, basil, garlic powder, oregano, and pepper; simmer about 25 minutes, stirring occasionally. Meanwhile, cook lasagna noodles according to package directions. Blend cottage cheese, eggs, spinach, and salt. Place thin layer of meat sauce in bottom of prepared casserole. Top with half the drained noodles, half the cottage cheese mixture, half the remaining meat sauce, and half the cheese. Repeat layers and sprinkle top with grated Parmesan cheese. Bake 30 minutes. Remove from oven and let stand 10 minutes before serving.
12 servings

STUFFED BEEF ROLLS WITH SHERRIED ASPARAGUS SAUCE

Sure to become a family favorite.

1 Tablespoon butter or margarine	4 beef top round butterfly steaks
1/3 cup finely chopped onion	2 Tablespoons vegetable shortening
1/3 cup finely chopped celery	1 can (10 3/4 ounces) condensed cream of asparagus soup, undiluted
1 clove garlic, minced	
1 1/2 cups soft bread crumbs	
3 Tablespoons grated Parmesan cheese	1/4 cup milk
1 Tablespoon chopped parsley	1 package (8 ounces) Frozen Stokely's® Asparagus Cuts & Tips
1 teaspoon marjoram	2 Tablespoons dry sherry (optional)
1/4 teaspoon sage	
1/8 teaspoon pepper	

Melt butter in small skillet. Add onion, celery, and garlic and sauté until onion is transparent. Remove from heat and place onion mixture in medium-size bowl. Add bread crumbs, cheese, parsley, marjoram, sage, and pepper to bowl and stir with fork until well combined. Divide mixture into 4 portions. Place 1 portion on each steak and roll steak, jelly-roll fashion; secure ends with short skewers, wooden toothpicks, or tie with string. Melt shortening in medium-size skillet and brown meat rolls well. Combine soup, milk, and asparagus; pour into skillet around meat. Cover and simmer 25 to 30 minutes, or until meat is tender. Add sherry before serving. Serve meat with asparagus sauce spooned over top.   *4 servings*

ROULADEN

Impress friends with this dish.

1 1/2 pounds round steak,
     1/2 inch thick
6 teaspoons Dijon mustard
6 thin slices ham, fully
     cooked
3 dill pickles, split
     lengthwise
1/4 cup vegetable shortening
2 cups Stokely's Finest®
     Tomato Juice

1/2 cup chopped onion
1/2 cup chopped celery
1 teaspoon instant beef
     flavored bouillon
2 Tablespoons cornstarch
1/4 cup water
1 cup commercial sour
     cream

Cut the round steak into 6 rectangular pieces. Pound to 1/4 inch thick. Spread each piece with 1 teaspoon mustard, top with ham, and place pickle at narrow end. Roll up, jelly-roll fashion. Secure with toothpicks or tie with string. Melt shortening in skillet and brown meat rolls on all sides. Add tomato juice, onion, celery, and bouillon; bring to a boil. Reduce heat; simmer, covered, 2 hours. Remove meat to serving dish. Blend cornstarch and water. Stir cornstarch mixture slowly into sauce in skillet. Heat to boiling, stirring constantly, and boil 1 minute. Remove from heat and slowly add the sour cream. Serve as a gravy with rouladen.   *6 servings*

KRAUT 'N BURGER BALLS

A favorite flavor combination.

1 pound lean ground beef
1/4 cup dry bread crumbs
1/4 cup chopped onion
1 teaspoon salt
1/4 teaspoon pepper
1 can (16 ounces)
     Stokely's Finest®
     Bavarian Style
     Sauerkraut, well drained

1/4 cup Stokely's Finest®
     Tomato Catsup
1 can (16 ounces)
     Stokely's Finest®
     Stewed Tomatoes
1/4 cup firmly packed brown
     sugar

Preheat oven to 350°F. Mix together ground beef, bread crumbs, onion, salt, and pepper; form into 8 meatballs. Place sauerkraut in a greased 1 1/2-quart casserole. Arrange meatballs on top of sauerkraut. Combine remaining ingredients, mix well, and pour over meatballs. Bake 1 hour.   *4 servings*

CORN-STUFFED ROUND STEAK

A different approach to round steak.

1 1/2 pounds boneless round
    steak
2 cups soft bread crumbs
1/2 cup chopped onion
1/3 cup chopped celery
2 Tablespoons
    Stokely's Finest®
    Sliced Pimientos,
    chopped
1 can (8 1/2 ounces)
    Stokely's Finest®
    Whole Kernel Golden
    Corn, drained

1 can (4 ounces)
    mushrooms, drained
    and chopped
1 teaspoon salt
1/8 teaspoon pepper
1/2 cup white port wine
1 beef flavored
    bouillon cube
    Dash seasoned salt
2 Tablespoons all-purpose
    flour

Preheat oven to 350°F. Trim excess fat from meat. Leaving the meat in one piece, pound with a mallet until it is about 1/4 inch thick. In a bowl, mix bread crumbs, onion, celery, pimientos, corn, mushrooms, salt, and pepper. Spread corn mixture on top of steak and roll up jelly-roll fashion. Tie at 1 1/2-inch intervals with string, or secure with skewers. Place roll in an 11×7×2-inch baking pan. Pour wine over meat and add bouillon cube to pan. Sprinkle with seasoned salt, cover, and bake 1 1/2 hours, basting 3 times with pan juices. When ready to serve, remove meat to a warm platter. Pour pan juices into a small saucepan, add flour, and blend well. Simmer about 5 minutes, or until sauce is thick. Slice meat and serve with sauce.   *5 servings*

APRICOT BEAN CASSEROLE

A tasty combination.

1 package (16 ounces)
    knackwurst
1 can (16 ounces)
    Van Camp's® Pork
    and Beans

1/4 cup apricot preserves
2 Tablespoons Stokely's
    Finest® Tomato Catsup
2 teaspoons chopped onion
1/4 teaspoon soy sauce

Preheat oven to 350°F. Split knackwurst in half lengthwise. Combine remaining ingredients and place in casserole. Nestle knackwurst into beans and bake, uncovered, 30 minutes.
4 servings

VEGETABLE PIE

Complete meal that travels well!

Pastry for 9-inch
2-crust pie
1 pound very lean ground
beef, divided into 3
parts
1 can (17 ounces)
Stokely's Finest®
Whole Kernel Golden
Corn, drained and
divided

1 can (8 ounces)
Stokely's Finest®
Sliced Carrots,
drained
1/2 cup chopped celery,
divided
1/3 cup chopped onion,
divided
Salt and pepper

Preheat oven to 450°F. In unbaked pastry shell place first layer of uncooked beef, top with half the corn, all the carrots, half the celery, and half the onion. Season with salt and pepper. Add the second layer of beef and the remaining vegetables. Top with third layer of beef, salt, and pepper. Place top crust over pie, sealing edges. Make slits in top crust to allow steam to escape. Bake 10 minutes; reduce heat to 350°F. and bake an additional 50 minutes.   *6 servings*

PEACHY BEAN CASSEROLE

Easy, saucy, and good.

1 can (16 ounces)
Van Camp's® Brown
Sugar Beans
2 Tablespoons
Stokely's Finest®
Tomato Catsup

1/4 cup peach preserves
2 Tablespoons chopped
onion
1/4 teaspoon soy sauce
4 chicken thighs or
breasts

Preheat oven to 350°F. Combine beans, catsup, preserves, onion, and soy sauce in a 10×6×2-inch baking dish. To coat chicken pieces evenly with sauce, nestle chicken in bean mixture, skin side down, then turn pieces skin side up; cover and bake 1 hour. Uncover and bake an additional 30 minutes, basting chicken with sauce occasionally.   *4 servings*

CASSEROLE MILANO

You'll serve this casserole often.

1/2 cup commercial sour cream

3 Tablespoons all-purpose flour

1/4 cup chopped onion

2 teaspoons prepared mustard

1 can (10 3/4 ounces) condensed cream of celery soup, undiluted

2 cups cooked ham, cut into 1/2-inch cubes

1 package (16 ounces) Frozen Stokely's® Vegetables Milano®

1/3 cup dry bread crumbs

2 Tablespoons grated Parmesan cheese

2 Tablespoons butter or margarine, melted

1/2 teaspoon paprika

Preheat oven to 350°F. Combine sour cream, flour, onion, mustard, and soup in 2-quart casserole, blending thoroughly. Stir in ham and vegetables, spreading mixture evenly in casserole. Mix bread crumbs, cheese, butter, and paprika; sprinkle over casserole. Bake, covered, 1 hour.   *4 servings*

Microwave Method: Combine sour cream, flour, onion, mustard, and soup in 2 1/2-quart covered casserole, blending thoroughly. Stir in ham and vegetables, spreading mixture evenly in casserole. Cover and microcook 15 minutes, stirring every 5 minutes (including just before topping is added). Mix bread crumbs, cheese, butter, and paprika; sprinkle over casserole and cook, uncovered, an additional 2 minutes.

Nice to know: Use a slightly larger casserole when you make a recipe in the microwave oven. That way you will have room to stir and food will cook more evenly.

Opposite: Casserole Milano, Cannelloni Supreme (page 78)

CHORIZO CASSEROLE

Olé!

1/2 of 16-ounce package
(8 ounces)
Frozen Stokely's®
Vegetables del Sol®
1/3 cup olive or vegetable
oil
2 large ripe tomatoes,
chopped

2 cloves garlic, crushed
1/2 teaspoon paprika
1 Tablespoon water
3 Tablespoons grated Edam
cheese
Butter or margarine
1 pound Spanish sausage
(chorizo), sliced

Preheat oven to 400°F. Cook vegetables according to package directions, drain, and spread evenly in 9-inch square baking dish; set aside. Combine olive oil, tomatoes, garlic, and paprika in saucepan. Cook 20 minutes over high heat, or until well blended. Add water; stir 1 minute. Pour over vegetables. Sprinkle with grated cheese, dot with butter, and lay sliced sausage on top. Bake 15 minutes, or until top is browned and cheese completely melted.   *4 servings*

TAMALE BEAN PIE

A nice way to dress up an old favorite.

1 can (31 ounces)
Van Camp's® Pork
and Beans
1 package (1 1/2 ounces)
Sloppy Joe seasoning
mix

1/2 cup Stokely's Finest®
Tomato Catsup
1/2 cup molasses
8 wieners, cut into
chunks

Corn Bread Topping:

3/4 cup cornmeal
1/4 cup all-purpose flour
1/2 teaspoon salt
1 1/2 teaspoons baking powder
1 Tablespoon sugar

1 egg
1/2 cup milk
3 Tablespoons vegetable
oil

Preheat oven to 350°F. Combine pork and beans, seasoning mix, catsup, molasses, and wieners in large casserole. Bake 20 minutes. Meanwhile, make corn bread topping. Sift dry ingredients together; blend in egg, milk, and oil. Pour batter over beans, increase oven temperature to 425°F., and bake 15 to 18 minutes.   *6 to 8 servings*

HOT DIGGETY DOG SKILLET

Quick — easy — economical — and delicious.

4 wieners, (about
8 ounces), sliced
2 Tablespoons butter or
margarine
2 Tablespoons
Stokely's Finest®
Tomato Catsup

1 can (15 ounces)
Van Camp's®
Spanish Rice
Grated Parmesan
cheese (optional)

Sauté wieners in butter until lightly browned. Add remaining ingredients except cheese; cover and heat to serving temperature. Sprinkle with Parmesan cheese before serving.   *4 servings*

APPLE-KRAUT BAVARIAN

A favorite! Serve with mashed potatoes and salad.

1 package (10 ounces)
brown and serve sausages
2 Tablespoons water
1 can (16 1/2 ounces)
Stokely's Finest®
Applesauce

1 can (16 ounces)
Stokely's Finest®
Bavarian Style
Sauerkraut, slightly
drained

Cook sausage in water until lightly browned, turning frequently. Stir in applesauce and sauerkraut. Heat to serving temperature.   *4 servings*

ORANGEY PORK AND BEANS

Marmalade provides a new taste treat.

1 can (16 ounces)
Van Camp's® Pork
and Beans
1/2 cup finely chopped onion,

1 cup cubed, cooked ham
1/2 cup orange marmalade
1/3 cup Stokely's Finest®
Tomato Catsup

Preheat oven to 350°F. Combine all ingredients and place in a 1 1/2-quart casserole. Bake, uncovered, 30 minutes. For thicker consistency, bake longer.   *4 servings*

KRAUT 'N CHOP BAKE

This is one of the best and easiest recipes of a classic dish.

6 pork chops
Salt and pepper
2 Tablespoons butter or
margarine (optional)
1 cup chopped onions
1 medium-size apple,
chopped

2 Tablespoons brown sugar
1 can (27 ounces)
Stokely's Finest®
Shredded Sauerkraut,
rinsed and drained
1/4 cup dry vermouth or
water

Preheat oven to 350°F. Trim excess fat from chops, season with salt and pepper and brown on both sides in skillet. Drain chops on paper towels and set aside. Drain all but 2 Tablespoons grease from skillet (or use butter if desired); add onion, apple, and brown sugar to skillet. Sauté until onion is transparent. Add sauerkraut and mix well. Transfer sauerkraut mixture to 2-quart casserole. Top with reserved chops. Add vermouth or water to skillet and scrape pan over high heat to release drippings. Pour over chops, cover, and bake 1 hour and 30 minutes, or until chops are tender.   *6 servings*

Slow Cook Method: Trim excess fat from chops, season with salt and pepper, and brown on both sides in skillet. Drain on paper towels and set aside. Drain all but 2 Tablespoons grease from skillet (or use butter if desired); add onion, apple, and brown sugar. Sauté until onion is transparent. Add sauerkraut and mix well. Transfer sauerkraut mixture to slow cooker. Bury chops in sauerkraut mixture. Add vermouth or water to skillet and scrape pan over high heat to release drippings. Pour over chops, cover and cook on low 8 to 10 hours or on high 3 to 4 hours.

Opposite: Kraut 'N Chop Bake, Hot Orange Gatorade® thirst quencher, Beans and Franks (page 64), Frozen Stokely's® Corn on the Cob

BEANS AND FRANKS

It's a tradition.

3 Tablespoons chopped
  onion
2 Tablespoons butter or
  margarine
1 can (31 ounces)
  Van Camp's® Pork
  and Beans

6 wieners, cut penny
  fashion
1/3 cup firmly packed brown
  sugar
1 teaspoon prepared
  mustard
1 teaspoon celery salt

Preheat oven to 350°F. Sauté onion in butter until transparent. Combine onion with remaining ingredients in 2-quart casserole. Bake, uncovered, 40 minutes, stirring occasionally.   *6 servings*

KRAUT-DOG BAKE

Serve with mashed potatoes for a hearty meal.

1/3 cup chopped onion
1 Tablespoon butter or
  margarine, melted
1 can (16 ounces)
  Stokely's Finest®
  Bavarian Style
  Sauerkraut, drained

2 Tablespoons brown sugar
4 wieners, slashed
  diagonally

In skillet, sauté onion in butter until transparent. Combine sauerkraut and brown sugar with onion in skillet. Top with wieners, cover and heat 20 minutes.   *4 servings*

TOTE ALONG BEAN BUNDLES

Ideal for a picnic.

8 large cabbage leaves
1 can (16 ounces)
  Van Camp's® Pork
  and Beans
1 package (10 ounces)
  brown and serve
  sausages, cut penny
  fashion

1/4 cup chopped onion
1/4 cup chopped green
  pepper
1 teaspoon
  Worcestershire sauce
Dash salt and pepper

Immerse cabbage leaves in boiling water for 3 minutes, or just until limp; drain. Slit heavy center vein of leaf about 2 inches. Combine the remaining ingredients. Place 1/8 bean mixture on each leaf. Fold in sides and ends; fasten with toothpicks. Steam bean bundles on rack in covered pan with small amount of water for 15 to 20 minutes.   *4 servings*

APPETIZING KRAUT

Serve with mashed potatoes. You'll love it!

3/4 cup beer
1/3 cup firmly packed brown
    sugar
  2 Tablespoons
    Stokely's Finest®
    Tomato Catsup
1/8 teaspoon barbecue spice

4 wieners, (about
    8 ounces) cut into
    bite-size pieces
1 can (16 ounces)
    Stokely's Finest®
    Chopped Sauerkraut,
    well drained

Combine beer, brown sugar, catsup, and barbecue spice in skillet. Add wieners and simmer 20 to 30 minutes, or until sauce thickens. Stir in sauerkraut and heat until bubbly hot.   *4 servings*

GERMAN PORK AND BEAN BAKE

A nice flavor combination.

1 can (31 ounces)
    Van Camp's® Pork
    and Beans
1 can (16 ounces)
    Stokely's Finest®
    Bavarian Style
    Sauerkraut, rinsed
    and drained
1 can (16 1/2 ounces)
    Stokely's Finest®
    Applesauce

1/3 cup chopped onion
1/2 cup firmly packed brown
    sugar
1/2 teaspoon dry mustard
1/2 teaspoon seasoned salt
  6 wieners

Preheat oven to 350°F. Combine all ingredients except wieners, in greased 2 1/2-quart casserole. Bake 25 minutes. Place wieners on top of bean mixture and bake an additional 20 minutes.
6 servings

BEAN TACOS

A delicious quick supper.

4 wieners, (about 8 ounces), cut penny fashion
1 can (21 ounces) Van Camp's® Pork and Beans
2 1/2 Tablespoons taco seasoning mix

1 1/2 cups shredded lettuce
1 1/2 cups corn chips, coarsely crushed
1/2 cup shredded American cheese

Combine wieners, pork and beans, and taco mix in saucepan. Simmer 5 minutes. Layer lettuce and corn chips on plate; spoon bean mixture over all and top with cheese.   *4 to 5 servings*

PORK AND PEACHES CHINESE STYLE

Try this different flavor treat.

1 1/2 pound pork loin cutlets
1 Tablespoon vegetable oil
2 cups sliced celery
3 scallions (green onions), sliced
2 large cloves garlic, minced
1 can (4 ounces) mushroom stems and pieces, drained
1 can (16 ounces) bean sprouts, drained

1 package (6 ounces) Chinese pea pods (frozen or fresh)
1 can (8 ounces) water chestnuts, drained and sliced
1 can (29 ounces) Stokely's Finest® Sliced Cling Peaches
1/3 cup soy sauce
2 Tablespoons cornstarch
1/2 teaspoon ginger
Cooked rice

Cut pork, against the grain, into thin 1/8-inch slices. Heat 10-inch skillet or wok over high heat; pour oil in wide, circular motion inside rim of pan. Tilt to coat surface, add pork, and stir-fry until meat is cooked through. Add celery, scallions, garlic, mushrooms, bean sprouts, pea pods, and water chestnuts. Cook about 5 minutes, stirring constantly. (Vegetables should remain crisp.) Reduce heat to medium. Drain peaches, reserving 1/2 cup liquid. Add soy sauce, cornstarch, and ginger to reserved liquid. Blend well. Pour sauce in middle of pan, tossing to cover vegetables and meat well. Cook until sauce thickens; add peaches. Simmer an additional 2 minutes. Serve over rice.   *6 to 8 servings*

PORK CHOPS AND PEAS WITH MUSHROOM SAUCE

Serve with buttered noodles.

6 pork chops
2 packages (10 ounces each)
    Frozen Stokely's®
    Green Peas
1/2 cup chopped onion

1 can (10 3/4 ounces)
    condensed cream of
    mushroom soup,
    undiluted
1/2 cup milk

Preheat oven to 350°F. Trim excess fat from chops and brown on both sides in skillet. Transfer chops to large, shallow baking dish. Combine peas, onion, soup, and milk in medium-size bowl and stir. Pour pea mixture over pork chops, cover, and bake 1 hour. Uncover and bake an additional 10 minutes, or until chops are tender.
6 servings

ITALIAN SKILLET

Serve spaghetti and red wine with this Italian dish.

1 pound bulk Italian
    sausage
1/4 cup chopped onion
1 can (15 ounces)
    Stokely's Finest®
    Dark Red Kidney Beans
1 can (8 ounces)
    Stokely's Finest®
    Tomato Sauce

1/4 teaspoon salt
1/4 teaspoon Italian
    seasoning
1/8 teaspoon garlic powder

Cook sausage in covered skillet about 10 minutes, turning occasionally. Drain excess fat. Add onion and cook until transparent. Stir in remaining ingredients and simmer, covered, 20 minutes.   *4 servings*

GLAZED PORK CHOPS

An attractive dish.

1 jar (16 ounces)
Stokely's Finest®
Tiny Whole Pickled
Beets
1/4 cup chopped onion
1/4 cup sugar
2 Tablespoons soy sauce

1 teaspoon instant beef
flavored bouillon
6 pork chops, cut
1/2-inch thick
2 Tablespoons cornstarch
2 Tablespoons water

Preheat oven to 325°F. Drain beet juice into oven-proof skillet. Stir in onion, sugar, soy sauce, and bouillon. Trim excess fat from chops and arrange in skillet, turning to moisten with liquid. Cover and bake 1 hour and 30 minutes, or until tender. Remove from oven and place chops on warm serving platter. Blend cornstarch with water and stir into skillet liquid. Heat on top of range until mixture thickens. Stir in pickled beets and heat to serving temperature. Serve with chops.   *6 servings*

PINWHEEL SAUSAGE BAKE

A favorite Austrian dish.

1 package (12 ounces)
pork sausage links
3 Tablespoons water
1 can (16 ounces)
Stokely's Finest®
Chopped Sauerkraut,
drained
1 cup commercial sour
cream

1/2 cup milk
2 Tablespoons butter or
margarine, melted
1 Tablespoon poppy seeds
1 teaspoon onion salt
1/4 teaspoon pepper
2 cups cooked noodles

Preheat oven to 375°F. Place sausage links and water in covered skillet and cook 5 minutes, turning frequently. Uncover skillet and cook 10 to 12 minutes longer, or until evenly browned. Meanwhile, combine remaining ingredients in 2-quart casserole. Drain sausage links and arrange, pinwheel fashion, on top of sauerkraut mixture. Bake 25 minutes.   *4 to 6 servings*

ALOHA SKILLET HOMINY

Pineapple adds a special new flavor.

1 package (10 ounces)
   brown and serve sausages
1/2 cup chopped onion
3 Tablespoons water
2 Tablespoons butter or
   margarine
1 can (20 ounces)
   Van Camp's® White
   Hominy, drained

1 can (8 1/4 ounces)
   crushed pineapple,
   drained
Dash dry mustard
Dash salt
1 Tablespoon chopped
   parsley

Simmer sausages, onion, and water in skillet until onion is transparent and sausages browned. Add butter and hominy and cook until hominy is heated through. Stir in pineapple, mustard, and salt; cook 2 to 3 minutes. Sprinkle with parsley.   *4 to 5 servings*

SKILLET RICE SUPPER

A "working woman's" answer to dinner!

1 package (16 ounces)
   wieners, cut penny
   fashion
1 Tablespoon butter or
   magarine
1 can (15 ounces)
   Van Camp's® Spanish
   Rice
1 can (16 ounces)
   Stokely's Finest®
   Cut Green Beans, drained

1/4 cup Stokely's Finest®
   Tomato Catsup
1/2 teaspoon seasoned salt
1 cup canned French-fried
   onions

In skillet, brown wieners in butter. Add Spanish rice, green beans, catsup, and salt. Simmer until heated through. Sprinkle onions on top and serve.   *4 servings*

COUNTRY-STYLE SAUERKRAUT AND SAUSAGES

Everyone will ask for seconds.

8 brown and serve sausages, cut into 1-inch pieces	2 Tablespoons brown sugar
1 Tablespoon butter or margarine	1 egg, beaten
1 can (16 ounces) Stokely's Finest® Bavarian Style Sauerkraut, well drained	2 Tablespoons grated onion
	2 1/2 cups prepared mashed potatoes

Preheat oven to 350°F. Brown sausages in butter over medium heat 5 to 6 minutes, turning frequently. Stir in sauerkraut and brown sugar and warm through. Pour into greased 2-quart casserole. Set aside. Add egg and onion to mashed potatoes, and stir well. Spread potato mixture over sauerkraut. Bake, uncovered, 25 minutes.
4 to 6 servings

PARISIAN SOUFFLÉ ROLL-UP

This recipe will confirm your reputation as a gourmet cook.

6 Tablespoons butter or margarine	6 eggs, separated
3/4 cup all-purpose flour	1 package (16 ounces) Frozen Stokely's® Vegetables Parisian™
3/4 teaspoon salt	
3 1/2 cups milk, divided	1/4 teaspoon dry mustard
1 1/2 cups shredded Swiss cheese, divided	

Preheat oven to 325°F. Grease a 15×10×1-inch jelly-roll pan, line with foil, and grease foil. Melt butter in medium-size saucepan; blend in flour and salt. Add 3 cups milk, stirring constantly until sauce thickens. Remove from heat, pour 1 cup sauce into small saucepan and reserve. Add 1/2 cup cheese to the remaining sauce and stir until cheese melts. Set aside to cool slightly.

Beat egg whites in a large bowl until soft peaks form. Set aside. Beat egg yolks in a large bowl until light and thick, about 3 minutes.

Stir a small amount of the hot cheese sauce into the yolks, then slowly add the remainder of the sauce and stir until mixture is well blended. Fold about a cup of the egg whites into the egg-yolk mixture (this will lighten the sauce). Fold sauce very gently into the remaining egg whites. Spread soufflé mixture evenly in prepared pan. Bake for 45 minutes, or until top is golden and springs back when touched. While soufflé bakes, cook vegetables according to package directions and drain well. To reserved sauce, add dry mustard, 1/2 cup cheese, and remaining 1/2 cup milk. Stir over low heat until cheese melts.

When soufflé is done, remove from oven and loosen around edges. Cover a cookie sheet with foil, place over soufflé, turn soufflé upside down; remove jelly-roll pan and layer of foil carefully. Spread vegetable mixture evenly over soufflé and sprinkle with remaining cheese. Pour 1/2 cup sauce over vegetables and cheese. Starting at the 10-inch side, roll jelly-roll fashion, lifting foil to help guide soufflé. Place on heated platter and spoon some of the remaining sauce over the top. Cut roll into thick slices and serve with sauce.   *8 servings*

JAPANESE STIR-FRY PORK

For variety, substitute chicken or beef for the pork.

1 **pound pork loin cutlets**	1 **package (14 ounces)**
2 **teaspoons cornstarch**	**Frozen Stokely's®**
1/2 **teaspoon sugar**	**Japanese Style**
2 **Tablespoons soy sauce**	**Stir-Fry Vegetables**
2 **Tablespoons vegetable**	1 **Tablespoon water**
oil, divided	

Cut pork against the grain into 1/8-inch slices. Combine cornstarch, sugar, and soy sauce. Add pork and toss to coat all pieces. Let stand to marinate 10 to 15 minutes. Heat 9- or 10-inch skillet or wok over high heat until very hot. Pour 1 Tablespoon oil in a wide, circular motion inside the rim of pan. Tilt pan to coat surface, add pork and stir-fry until pork turns white. Push meat to sides. Remove seasoning packet from vegetables and reserve; add vegetables to pan. Add remaining Tablespoon oil in circular motion. Cover and cook 3 minutes. Sprinkle reserved seasoning packet over mixture and add water. Cook and stir until vegetables are crisp-tender. Serve immediately.   *4 to 6 servings*

PARISIAN DINNER

An easy meal-in-a-dish.

4 slices bacon
6 wieners, cut into
   1-inch pieces
1 package (16 ounces)
   Frozen Stokely's®
   Vegetables Parisian™
1 can (15 ounces)
   Stokely's Finest®
   Small Peeled Whole
   White Potatoes,
   drained and sliced
   (optional)

1 can (10 3/4 ounces)
   condensed cream of
   celery soup,
   undiluted
1/4 cup milk
1/8 teaspoon pepper
1 cup cubed American
   cheese

Preheat oven to 350°F. Cook bacon in skillet until crisp; drain on paper towels, crumble, and reserve. Place wieners, vegetables, and potatoes in 2 1/2-quart casserole. Combine soup, milk, pepper, and cheese in bowl. Stir soup mixture into casserole. Cover and bake 30 minutes. Uncover casserole, sprinkle top with reserved bacon and bake an additional 5 minutes.   *6 to 8 servings*

Microwave Method: Place bacon between paper towels and microcook 2 to 3 minutes, or until crisp. Remove bacon, crumble, and reserve. Place wieners, vegetables, and potatoes in 2 1/2-quart casserole. Combine soup, milk, and pepper in bowl. Stir soup mixture into casserole. Cover and microcook 16 to 18 minutes, stirring twice. Add cheese and microcook, uncovered, an additional 2 minutes; stir to distribute cheese. Top with reserved bacon.

BROCCOLI ROLL-UPS

Ideal for brunch.

1 package (10 ounces)
   Frozen Stokely's®
   Broccoli Spears

6 slices boiled ham
1 cup favorite cheese
   sauce recipe

Preheat oven to 325°F. Prepare broccoli according to package directions. Drain and divide broccoli into 6 equal portions. Place 1 portion on each slice of ham and roll log fashion. Place filled logs in shallow baking dish; cover with aluminum foil and warm in oven for about 10 minutes, or until ham is warm. Serve 2 ham rolls per plate and top with cheese sauce.   *3 servings*

Nice to know: Frozen asparagus spears may be substituted for broccoli spears.

APPLE-SAUSAGE SKILLET

Perfect to serve after football practice.

1 **package (10 ounces) brown and serve sausages, cut into thirds**
1 **medium-size Delicious apple, cored and cut into chunks**
2 **Tablespoons butter or margarine**

1/4 **cup firmly packed brown sugar**
1 **can (15 ounces) Van Camp's® New Orleans Style Red Kidney Beans, drained**

Brown sausages with apple chunks in butter until apples are crispy tender. Stir in remaining ingredients and heat to serving temperature.   *4 servings*

SMOKED SAUSAGE DINNER

A German treat.

4 **Tablespoons butter or margarine**
1 **package (28 ounces) Frozen Stokely's® Size Wize® Vegetables Sized for Roast**

Seasoned salt
Pepper
1 **pound smoked sausage**

Preheat oven to 350°F. Melt butter in a 4-quart Dutch oven. Add frozen vegetables; season with salt and pepper. Top with sausage that has been split lengthwise. Cover and bake 1 hour and 30 minutes, or until vegetables are tender. Remove cover, place sausage and vegetables on serving platter. Pour pan juices over all and serve immediately. Garnish with parsley, if desired.
4 servings

SAUERKRAUT AND SPARERIBS

Dressed up spareribs.

2 pounds country-style
spareribs
1 cup water
1 can (27 ounces)
Stokely's Finest®
Shredded Sauerkraut

1 medium-size onion,
chopped
2 Tablespoons sugar
4 medium-size potatoes,
quartered

Preheat oven to 350°F. Place ribs in a 13×9×2-inch pan with water. Cover with foil and bake 1 hour. Discard foil and liquid surrounding ribs; set ribs aside. Combine sauerkraut, onion, and sugar. Place sauerkraut mixture over ribs; top with potatoes. Cover with foil and bake 1 hour.   *4 servings*

Slow Cook Method: Broil ribs 5 minutes on each side. Combine sauerkraut, onion, and sugar in slow cooker. Add 1/2 cup water, potatoes, and ribs; stir well. Cover and cook on low 8 to 10 hours or on high 5 to 6 hours.

ZIPPY PORK AND BEANS

Easy and unusual.

1 can (31 ounces)
Van Camp's® Pork
and Beans
3/4 pound kielbasa, sliced
1/4 cup firmly packed
brown sugar
1/4 cup chopped onion
1/4 cup Stokely's Finest®
Tomato Catsup

2 Tablespoons chopped
green pepper
1/4 teaspoon chili powder
5 Mexican pickles with
1 Tablespoon liquid
Dash garlic powder
1/8 teaspoon cumin

Preheat oven to 350°F. Place all ingredients in a 2-quart casserole. Mix well. Cover and bake 35 minutes.   *10 to 12 servings*

Microwave Method: Place all ingredients in a 2-quart casserole. Cover and microcook 10 minutes, stirring twice.

GREEN BEAN DIVAN

Excellent made with either chicken or turkey.

6 Tablespoons butter or margarine, melted
6 Tablespoons all-purpose flour
1 1/2 cups chicken broth
1/2 cup milk
3 Tablespoons dry sherry
1/2 teaspoon salt
Dash pepper

2/3 cup Parmesan cheese, divided
2 cans (16 ounces each) Stokely's Finest® Cut Green Beans, well drained
2 cups cubed cooked chicken breast

Preheat oven to 375°F. Blend butter and flour in saucepan. Stir in broth and milk. Cook and stir over medium heat until mixture bubbles and thickens. Remove from heat and stir in sherry, salt, pepper, and 1/3 cup cheese. Place half the beans in 2-quart casserole. Top with half the sauce, all the chicken, the remaining beans, and remaining sauce. Sprinkle with remaining 1/3 cup cheese and bake 15 minutes.   *5 to 6 servings*

CHICKEN BREASTS SUPREME

Sure to become a favorite.

2 cans (16 ounces each) Stokely's Finest® Sliced French Style Green Beans, drained
2 whole chicken breasts, halved, skinned, and boned
Seasoned salt
Paprika
1 can (10 3/4 ounces) condensed cream of mushroom soup, undiluted

1/3 cup Sauterne wine
1 cup grated American cheese
1 teaspoon parsley flakes
1 jar (2 ounces) Stokely's Finest® Sliced Pimientos, drained

Preheat oven to 350°F. Place green beans in greased 2 1/2-quart casserole or baking dish. Arrange chicken pieces on top of beans; sprinkle with salt and paprika. Combine soup with Sauterne; pour over chicken and beans. Sprinkle grated cheese, parsley flakes, and pimiento on top. Bake, covered, 1 hour. Uncover and bake an additional 30 minutes.   *4 servings*

OVEN CHICKEN STEW

A good meal with little effort.

1 package (20 ounces)
  Frozen Stokely's®
  Size Wize® Vegetables
  Sized for Stew
  Seasoned salt
2 1/2· to 3-pound
  chicken, cut into
  serving pieces
  Paprika
1 can (10 3/4 ounces)
  condensed cream of
  mushroom soup,
  undiluted

1/3 cup Sauterne wine
1 cup grated American
  cheese
1 teaspoon parsley flakes
1 jar (2 ounces)
  Stokely's Finest®
  Sliced Pimientos,
  drained and chopped

Preheat oven to 325°F. Place vegetables in greased 2 1/2-quart casserole. Sprinkle with seasoned salt. Arrange chicken on top of vegetables. Sprinkle with seasoned salt and paprika. Combine soup and wine; pour over chicken and vegetables. Sprinkle cheese, parsley flakes, and pimientos over top. Additional paprika may be added. Cover and bake 1 hour and 30 minutes. Remove cover and bake an additional 15 minutes.   *6 to 8 servings*

CRISPY CHICKEN WITH PEACH CUPS

Light and nutritious.

4 Tablespoons butter or
  margarine
2 whole chicken breasts,
  halved
1 cup crushed potato chips

1 can (16 ounces)
  Stokely's Finest®
  Cling Peach Halves
2/3 cup cottage cheese

Preheat oven to 325°F. Melt butter in 9-inch square pan. Place chicken pieces in melted butter, then turn pieces over to coat all sides. Put crushed potato chips in plastic bag. Add chicken to bag and shake to coat evenly. Place chicken pieces back in pan and bake, uncovered, 1 hour and 10 minutes. Drain peaches well and place cup side up alongside chicken in pan. Bake 5 minutes longer to warm through. Arrange chicken pieces on platter. Surround with peach halves filled with cold cottage cheese.   *4 servings*

CRUNCHY CHICKEN CASSEROLE

A quick way to use leftover chicken or turkey.

1 can (17 ounces)
  Stokely's Finest®
  Peas, drained
2 cups cubed cooked
  chicken
2 cups sliced celery
1 cup mayonnaise

2 Tablespoons lemon juice
2 teaspoons grated onion
1/2 cup grated pasteurized
  process American
  cheese
1/2 cup crushed potato
  chips

Preheat oven to 425°F. Combine peas, chicken, celery, mayonnaise, lemon juice, and onion in greased 1 1/2-quart casserole. Sprinkle with cheese, then with potato chips. Bake 20 minutes.   *6 servings*

PLAN-OVER TURKEY CASSEROLE

Chicken may be substituted for turkey.

1/3 cup chopped celery
1 Tablespoon butter or
  margarine
1 can (17 ounces)
  Stokely's Finest®
  Whole Kernel Golden
  Corn

1/3 cup mayonnaise
1/3 cup commercial sour
  cream
2 cups diced cooked turkey
1 teaspoon parsley flakes

Preheat oven to 350°F. Sauté celery in butter until tender. Drain corn reserving 2 Tablespoons corn liquid; add corn to celery and cook until heated through. Combine mayonnaise, sour cream, and reserved corn liquid. Fold into corn mixture. Place turkey in greased 1 1/2-quart casserole and top with corn mixture. Sprinkle with parsley. Bake 15 minutes.   *4 servings*

Microwave Method: Place celery and butter in 1 1/2-quart casserole. Cover and microcook 2 minutes. Drain corn reserving 2 Tablespoons corn liquid; add corn to celery, cover, and microcook 4 minutes, stirring after 2 minutes. Combine mayonnaise, sour cream, and reserved corn liquid; fold into corn mixture. Add turkey and stir to combine. Sprinkle with parsley, cover, and microcook 3 minutes longer, or until turkey is heated through.

CHICKEN 'N PEACHES POLYNESIAN

Delicious served over rice.

2 Tablespoons vegetable shortening
2 whole chicken breasts, halved
1 can (8 ounces) Stokely's Finest® Tomato Sauce
3/4 cup chicken broth
2 Tablespoons orange marmalade

1/4 cup chopped onion
2 Tablespoons soy sauce
1/4 teaspoon ginger
1/2 of 16-ounce package (8 ounces) Frozen Stokely's® Sliced Peaches
1/2 cup toasted slivered almonds

Melt shortening in large skillet and brown chicken well on both sides. Drain excess fat. Combine tomato sauce, chicken broth, marmalade, onion, soy sauce, and ginger in small saucepan. Cook over low heat, stirring until marmalade dissolves. Pour tomato sauce mixture over chicken, cover, and simmer 40 minutes. Meanwhile, cut each peach slice into thirds. Stir peaches into chicken and simmer, uncovered, an additional 10 to 15 minutes. Sprinkle with almonds and serve.   *4 servings*

CANNELLONI SUPREME

Make an extra batch to keep in your freezer.

2 Tablespoons butter or margarine
1 cup milk
2 eggs, well beaten
1/2 cup sifted all-purpose flour
1 teaspoon baking powder
1/2 teaspoon salt
1 package (16 ounces) Frozen Stokely's® Broccoli Florentine®

1/2 pound ground pork
1 cup finely chopped cooked chicken
1/4 cup grated Romano or Parmesan cheese
1/8 teaspoon thyme
Salt and pepper to taste

Sauce:

3 Tablespoons butter or margarine
3 Tablespoons all-purpose flour

1 1/2 cups half-and-half
1/2 cup grated Parmesan cheese
White pepper to taste

Melt butter in milk. Cool slightly. Add eggs, flour, baking powder, and salt and mix until smooth. Drop by Tablespoonfuls into hot buttered skillet (makes about sixteen 5-inch pancakes). Fry each pancake on both sides until browned; remove and set aside to cool. Prepare broccoli according to package directions. Drain and set aside. Brown pork in skillet; drain excess fat. Combine broccoli, pork, chicken, cheese, thyme, salt, and pepper. Spoon 2 Tablespoons of mixture in center of each pancake. Roll and put in shallow baking dish, seam side up.

Sauce: In small saucepan, melt butter and blend in flour. Gradually stir in half-and-half and continue stirring until mixture is thickened. Stir in Parmesan cheese. Adjust seasoning and pour over filled cannelloni. Broil about 5 minutes, or until browned and heated through.   *4 to 6 servings*

NEXT DAY CASSEROLE

A dish to enjoy the day after Thanksgiving.

1 can (10 3/4 ounces) condensed cream of chicken soup, undiluted	1/2 of 16-ounce package Frozen Stokely's® Vegetables del Sol®
1/2 cup mayonnaise or salad dressing	1/2 cup grated American cheese
1/2 teaspoon lemon juice	1/4 cup butter or margarine, melted
1/4 teaspoon curry powder	1 cup crushed cornflakes
2 cups cubed cooked turkey or chicken	1 teaspoon parsley flakes

Preheat oven to 350°F. Thoroughly blend soup, mayonnaise, lemon juice, and curry powder in 2-quart casserole. Stir in turkey and vegetables; sprinkle with cheese. Combine butter, cornflakes, and parsley flakes; spread over casserole. Bake 45 minutes.
6 to 8 servings

Microwave Method: Thoroughly blend soup, mayonnaise, lemon juice, and curry powder in 2 1/2-quart casserole. Stir in turkey and vegetables. Cover and microcook 10 minutes; stir after 5 minutes. Stir again and sprinkle with cheese. Combine butter, cornflakes, and parsley flakes; spread over casserole. Microcook, uncovered, 5 minutes.

CHICKEN À LA KING

Traditional, reliable, and always a favorite.

1 large whole chicken
   breast
1/4 teaspoon salt
2 cups water
   Milk
3 Tablespoons butter or
   margarine
3 Tablespoons all-purpose
   flour
1 teaspoon Worcestershire
   sauce
1 Tablespoon instant
   minced onion
1 package (10 ounces)
   Frozen Stokely's®
   Green Peas, cooked
   and drained

1 can (4 1/2 ounces)
   sliced mushrooms,
   drained
1 jar (2 ounces)
   Stokely's Finest®
   Sliced Pimientos,
   well drained
   Salt and pepper to
   taste
1 package (10 ounces)
   frozen patty shells,
   baked according to
   package directions

Place chicken in medium-size saucepan, add salt and water. Cover and simmer 45 minutes. Remove chicken and set aside to cool, reserving liquid. When chicken is cool, remove skin and bones, dice, and reserve. Add enough milk to reserved liquid to make 2 cups liquid. Melt butter over low heat, add flour, and cook until bubbly, stirring constantly. Pour reserved liquid in gradually, stirring constantly until thickened. Add Worcestershire and stir. Bring sauce to a boil, lower heat, add onion, peas, mushrooms, pimientos, salt, pepper, and diced chicken. Simmer until heated through. Spoon into prepared patty shells and serve.   *6 servings*

Nice to know: You can also use leftover cooked chicken or turkey. You may also use chopped hard-cooked eggs instead of mushrooms.

CHICKEN ORIENT WITH CASHEWS

A quick, easy dinner — oriental style.

3 Tablespoons vegetable oil
2 whole chicken breasts, skinned, boned, and cut into 1/2-inch wide strips or 4 chicken cutlets, cut into 1/2-inch wide strips
1 clove garlic, minced
2 teaspoons cornstarch
1/2 cup water

1 package (16 ounces) Frozen Stokely's® Vegetables Orient®
2 Tablespoons soy sauce
1/2 cup chopped dry roasted cashew nuts
1/2 teaspoon ginger
1 can (16 ounces) bean sprouts, drained

Heat oil in large skillet; add chicken and garlic and sauté until chicken turns white. Combine cornstarch and water; add to skillet with vegetables, soy sauce, nuts, and ginger; bring to boil. Lower heat, cover, and simmer 5 minutes, stirring occasionally. Add bean sprouts and simmer an additional 1 to 2 minutes. Serve immediately.   *4 servings*

BUTTER BEAN CHICKEN CASSEROLE

High in protein, high in flavor!

1 can (15 ounces) Van Camp's® Butter Beans
1/4 cup Stokely's Finest® Tomato Catsup
1 cup cubed cooked chicken
1/4 cup chopped green pepper

1 teaspoon instant minced onion
1/2 teaspoon Worcestershire sauce
Shredded Cheddar cheese
1/2 can (3 ounces) French-fried onion rings

Preheat oven to 325°F. In a 1-quart casserole place beans, catsup, chicken, green pepper, onion, and Worcestershire sauce. Bake, uncovered, 20 minutes. Top with desired amount of cheese and onion rings. Bake until cheese melts and onion rings are crisp.   *4 servings*

MOM'S DELECTABLE CHICKEN

Great served with oven-browned potatoes.

2 chicken breasts, halved
2 Tablespoons vegetable oil
1 small onion, sliced
1 can (16 ounces) Stokely's Finest® Sliced French Style Green Beans, drained

Salt and pepper
1/2 teaspoon garlic powder
1 can (16 ounces) Stokely's Finest® Stewed Tomatoes
1 1/2 cups shredded Cheddar cheese (about)

Preheat oven to 350°F. Brown chicken in oil. Remove chicken and sauté onion in drippings until transparent. Place green beans in a 3-quart oblong casserole. Top with chicken pieces and onion. Season with salt and pepper. Add garlic powder to tomatoes and pour over chicken. Bake, covered, 30 minutes. Uncover and bake an additional 30 minutes. Top each chicken piece with desired amount of cheese and bake an additional 15 minutes, or until cheese melts.   *4 servings*

SAUCY CHICKEN CASSEROLE

Elegant, make ahead dish.

3 whole chicken breasts, cooked and cubed
1 cup cooked rice
2 Tablespoons instant minced onion
1 can (10 3/4 ounces) condensed cream of mushroom soup, undiluted
1/2 cup commercial sour cream

1 can (4 ounces) mushroom stems and pieces, drained
1/2 cup sliced water chestnuts
1 can (17 ounces) Stokely's Finest® Peas, drained
1 cup crushed potato chips

Preheat oven to 350°F. Grease a shallow 8-inch square casserole. In large bowl place chicken, rice, onion, and soup; blend together. Gently fold in sour cream, mushrooms, water chestnuts, and peas. Spread mixture in casserole. Cover and bake 30 minutes. Sprinkle potato chips over top and bake, uncovered, an additional 10 minutes.   *8 servings*

PECAN CHICKEN 'N BROCCOLI

Try this special dish when company is coming.

4 Tablespoons dry sherry
3 Tablespoons soy sauce
1/2 teaspoon ginger
3 whole chicken breasts, halved, skinned, boned, and cut into 1-inch pieces
4 Tablespoons vegetable oil
1/4 cup sliced scallions (green onions)
2 cloves garlic, finely minced
1 package (10 ounces) Frozen Stokely's® Chopped Broccoli
1 cup chopped pecans

Combine sherry, soy sauce, and ginger in medium-size bowl. Add chicken and toss to coat; let stand 30 minutes to marinate. Drain chicken, reserving marinade. Heat oil in large skillet, add chicken and sauté over high heat until meat turns white, about 6 minutes. Remove chicken from skillet and set aside. Add scallions, garlic, broccoli, and pecans and cook over high heat 3 minutes, stirring constantly. Add reserved marinade and reserved chicken, toss lightly and simmer an additional 3 minutes, or until heated through. Serve immediately.   *6 servings*

EASY BARBECUE CHICKEN CASSEROLE

Sweet and special.

1 can (16 ounces) Van Camp's® Pork and Beans
4 pieces of chicken (thighs, breasts, or drumsticks)
1/4 cup Stokely's Finest® Tomato Catsup
2 Tablespoons peach preserves
2 teaspoons instant minced onion
1/4 teaspoon soy sauce
1/4 cup firmly packed brown sugar

Preheat oven to 325°F. Place pork and beans in 2-quart casserole. Top with chicken. Combine remaining ingredients and pour over chicken and beans. Cover and bake 1 hour and 45 minutes.   *4 servings*

HOT CHICKEN COCKTAIL SALAD

A special chicken treat.

2 whole chicken breasts
1 teaspoon salt
4 cups boiling water
1/2 cup mayonnaise or salad
    dressing
2 Tablespoons lemon juice
1/2 teaspoon poultry
    seasoning
1/2 teaspoon seasoned salt
    Dash pepper

1 can (30 ounces)
    Stokely's Finest®
    Fruit Cocktail,
    well drained
1/2 cup chopped celery
1/2 cup slivered blanched
    almonds, toasted
1/2 cup cracker crumbs
2 Tablespoons butter or
    margarine, melted

Simmer chicken in salted water 50 minutes, or until fork tender. Debone chicken and cut into 1/2-inch chunks. Preheat oven to 350°F. Combine chicken, mayonnaise, lemon juice, poultry seasoning, salt, and pepper; mix until chicken is coated. Gently fold in fruit cocktail, celery, and almonds. Place in 1 1/2-quart baking dish. Combine cracker crumbs and butter; sprinkle over top. Bake 20 minutes.   *6 to 8 servings*

Nice to know: Two cups cubed cooked turkey breast may be substituted for chicken.

CHINESE CHICKEN WITH CHERRIES

Sweet cherries provide a sweet-tart flavor treat.

2 whole boned, skinned
    chicken breasts
1/2 cup sugar
2 Tablespoons cornstarch
2 Tablespoons plus 1
    teaspoon lemon juice
2 Tablespoons water
2 Tablespoons vegetable
    oil, divided

1 package (14 ounces)
    Frozen Stokely's®
    Chinese Style
    Stir-Fry Vegetables
1 cup Frozen Stokely's®
    Dark Sweet Cherries,
    thawed
    Soy sauce

Cut chicken into 1-inch cubes. Combine sugar, cornstarch, lemon juice, and water; blend until smooth. Set aside. Heat 9- or 10-inch skillet or wok over high heat (a drop of water will sizzle). Pour 1

Tablespoon oil in wide, circular motion inside rim of pan. Tilt pan to coat surface; add chicken and stir-fry about 1 1/2 minutes, or until chicken turns white. Push chicken to side. Remove seasoning packet from vegetables and reserve; add frozen vegetables to pan. Pour remaining oil around rim of pan quickly. Toss vegetables to coat each piece. Cover and cook 3 minutes, stirring once midway. If vegetables begin to stick, reduce temperature slightly or add 1 teaspoon oil. Sprinkle reserved seasoning packet over mixture and blend. Cook about 30 seconds more. Push vegetables and meat to sides. Give reserved sauce a quick stir and pour into center of pan. When it comes to a boil, stir in vegetables and chicken. Add cherries; stir, remove from heat, and serve with soy sauce.   *4 servings*

CHICKEN AND SHRIMP ROYALE

Great way to use leftover chicken.

3 Tablespoons butter or margarine
3 Tablespoons all-purpose flour
1 1/2 cups milk
3/4 cup grated Gruyère or Swiss cheese
1 teaspoon Worcestershire sauce
Dash cayenne pepper
2 cups diced cooked cold chicken
1 package (10 ounces) Frozen Stokely's® Peas and Carrots, cooked and drained

1 can (4 1/2 ounces) deveined shrimp, drained and rinsed
1 jar (2 ounces) Stokely's Finest® Sliced Pimientos, well drained
2 Tablespoons dry white wine or vermouth
Cooked noodles or rice
1 Tablespoon fresh parsley (optional)

Melt butter in medium-size saucepan. Add flour, stirring to make smooth paste. Cook until bubbly. Gradually pour in milk, stirring constantly until thickened. Remove from heat, add cheese, Worcestershire, and cayenne, and stir until cheese is melted. Return saucepan to low heat, add chicken, vegetables, shrimp, and pimientos; stir. Add wine; stir, and cook 1 minute over low heat. Serve over hot noodles or rice. Garnish with parsley.   *4 servings*

ASPARAGUS LUNCHEON

So easy and so-o-o good!

1 package (8 ounces)
   Frozen Stokely's®
   Asparagus Cuts and Tips
1/2 cup soft bread crumbs
1 Tablespoon butter or
   margarine, melted
3/4 cup commercial sour
   cream
3/4 teaspoon prepared
   mustard

1 teaspoon lemon juice
1/4 teaspoon salt
2 English muffins, split
   and toasted
   Slices of cooked
   chicken, turkey, or
   ham
1 tomato

Cook asparagus according to package directions; drain and set aside. Brown bread crumbs in butter until golden; set aside. In small saucepan blend sour cream, mustard, lemon juice, and salt; warm gently, but do not boil. On individual serving plates, place 2 toasted muffin halves. Top each serving with a slice of meat, a slice of tomato, half the asparagus and half the sauce. Garnish with crumbs.   *2 servings*

TUNA JAPANESE

A new way to serve hot tuna fish.

1 can (6 1/2 ounces)
   chunk light tuna
   in water, well drained
5 Tablespoons soy sauce
1 teaspoon prepared
   horseradish

1 package (14 ounces)
   Frozen Stokely's®
   Japanese Style
   Stir-Fry Vegetables
1 Tablespoon vegetable
   oil

Place tuna in bowl and break into chunks. Combine soy sauce and horseradish and pour over tuna. Cover and refrigerate 30 minutes. Heat skillet over high heat until very hot. Remove seasoning packet from vegetables and reserve. Spread frozen vegetables evenly in hot skillet. Pour oil in wide, circular motion inside rim of pan; stir into vegetables, coating each piece. Cover and cook 3 minutes, stirring once midway. If vegetables begin to stick, reduce temperature slightly or add 1 teaspoon oil. Drain tuna, reserving 1 Tablespoon soy sauce mixture. Add tuna to vegetables; add seasoning packet and reserved soy sauce in same manner as oil. Cook and stir about 1 minute. Serve immediately.   *4 servings*

PEAS 'N SALMON LOAF

Quick and delicious.

1 can (15 1/2 ounces)
  salmon, drained and
  flaked
2 eggs, beaten
1 Tablespoon chopped onion
2 teaspoons lemon juice
1/2 teaspoon salt

1/2 cup fine cracker crumbs
1 can (8 1/2 ounces)
  Stokely's Finest® Peas,
  drained
1/4 cup Stokely's Finest®
  Tomato Catsup

Preheat oven to 350°F. Combine salmon, eggs, onion, lemon juice, salt, and cracker crumbs in mixing bowl. Carefully fold in peas. Pack into greased 1 1/2-quart loaf pan and bake 30 minutes. Spread loaf with catsup and bake an additional 5 minutes.   *4 servings*

EASY FISH CASSEROLE

Fish and vegetables in mushroom sauce.

1 package (14 1/2 ounces)
  frozen French-fried
  halibut (breaded or
  batter dipped)
1 package (8 ounces)
  wide egg noodles
1 package (10 ounces)
  Frozen Stokely's®
  Mixed Vegetables
1 can (10 3/4 ounces)
  condensed cream of
  mushroom soup,
  undiluted

1 cup commercial sour
  cream
1/2 cup half-and-half
  or milk
2 teaspoons Worcestershire
  sauce
1/2 teaspoon onion powder
  Salt and pepper to
  taste

Bake halibut according to package directions; also cook noodles and vegetables according to directions on each package. Preheat oven to 350°F. Meanwhile, combine remaining ingredients in a shallow 2-quart casserole. Drain noodles and vegetables; add to casserole and stir to combine. Bake 20 minutes. Remove dish from oven, place fish on top, and bake, uncovered, an additional 10 minutes, or until heated through.   *4 servings*

SEASIDE CASSEROLE

Peas and seafood with a Chinese touch.

1 medium-size onion, chopped	2 cans (6 1/2 ounces each) chunk light tuna in water, well drained
3 Tablespoons butter or margarine, melted	1 can (17 ounces) Stokely's Finest® Peas, drained
1 can (10 3/4 ounces) condensed cream of shrimp soup, undiluted	1/2 cup commercial sour cream
1 can (8 ounces) water chestnuts, drained and sliced	Salt and pepper to taste
1/2 cup milk	Chow mein noodles

Sauté onion in butter until tender. Stir in soup, water chestnuts, milk, and tuna; bring mixture to a boil. Gently fold in peas and sour cream; season with salt and pepper. Heat to serving temperature and serve over chow mein noodles.   *6 servings*

SHRIMP SALAD PARISIAN

A summertime treat.

1 package (16 ounces) Frozen Stokely's® Vegetables Parisian™	3 cups assorted lettuce, torn
1 cup frozen cooked cocktail shrimp	Thousand Island dressing

Allow vegetables to defrost at room temperature in colander about 3 hours. Defrost shrimp according to package directions. Wash and dry lettuce. Line the salad bowl with assorted lettuce and top with vegetables and shrimp. Serve with Thousand Island dressing.   *4 servings*

Vegetables

BARBECUED GREEN BEANS

A yummy southern recipe.

2 slices bacon
1 medium-size onion,
   sliced
1/4 cup Stokely's Finest®
   Tomato Catsup
1/4 cup firmly packed
   brown sugar

1 can (16 ounces)
   Stokely's Finest®
   Whole Green Beans,
   drained

Preheat oven to 350°F. Cook bacon until crisp. Drain bacon on paper towel, crumble, and set aside. Sauté onion in drippings until transparent. Drain. Stir catsup and brown sugar together. Place green beans in a 2-quart casserole. Pour tomato mixture over beans, add bacon and onion. Cover and bake 1 hour.   *3 to 4 servings*

Microwave Method: In casserole, microcook bacon, covered, 3 to 5 minutes, or until bacon is crisp. Drain drippings and crumble bacon. Add bacon, onion, catsup, and brown sugar to casserole; mix thoroughly. Add green beans, cover, and microcook 7 minutes, stirring twice.

COMPANY VEGETABLE CASSEROLE

Cheese crackers add an unusual topping.

1 can (17 ounces)
  Stokely's Finest®
  Whole Kernel
  White Corn,
  drained
1 can (16 ounces)
  Stokely's Finest®
  Sliced French Style
  Green Beans, drained
1 can (10 3/4 ounces)
  condensed cream of
  celery soup,
  undiluted

1 cup grated sharp Cheddar
  cheese
1/2 cup commercial sour
  cream
1/2 cup chopped celery
1/2 cup chopped onion
1/4 cup chopped green pepper
3/4 cup cheese-flavored
  cracker crumbs
2 Tablespoons butter or
  margarine, melted

Preheat oven to 325°F. Combine corn, green beans, soup, cheese, sour cream, celery, onion, and green pepper in greased 2-quart casserole and bake 30 minutes. Blend cracker crumbs and butter and sprinkle over casserole. Bake an additional 10 minutes.   *8 to 10 servings*

Variation:

Substitute 1 can (17 ounces) Stokely's Finest® Whole Kernel Golden Corn for White Corn.

CHEDDAR ZUCCHINI SUPREME

Everyone loves this.

2 Tablespoons butter or
  margarine
6 cups thinly sliced
  fresh zucchini
1 teaspoon salt
1/8 teaspoon pepper

Dash garlic salt
1 can (8 ounces)
  Stokely's Finest®
  Tomato Sauce
1 cup shredded Cheddar
  cheese, divided

Preheat oven to 375°F. Melt butter in medium-size skillet. Add zucchini, salt, pepper, garlic salt, and tomato sauce. Heat 10 minutes, stirring occasionally. Add 1/2 cup cheese, and stir until cheese is melted. Pour into greased 1 1/2-quart casserole. Sprinkle with remaining cheese and bake 20 minutes.   *6 servings*

RANCH HOUSE BEANS

A Texas favorite.

1/4 pound bacon
2 cans (15 ounces each) Stokely's Finest® Light Red Kidney Beans, drained
1/3 cup maple syrup
1 can (8 ounces) Stokely's Finest® Tomato Sauce

1 small onion, minced
3/4 teaspoon garlic salt
3/4 teaspoon seasoned salt
1/2 teaspoon chili powder
1/4 cup Parmesan cheese

Preheat oven to 350°F. Cook bacon in skillet until crisp; drain bacon on paper towels; crumble and reserve. Combine remaining ingredients except Parmesan cheese in 1 1/2-quart casserole; mix well. Cover and bake 40 minutes, or until hot and bubbly. Remove cover, sprinkle with reserved bacon and cheese and bake, uncovered, an additional 10 minutes.   *6 to 8 servings*

BROCCOLI CHEESE CASSEROLE

A company favorite.

1 package (10 ounces) Frozen Stokely's® Chopped Broccoli
2/3 cup condensed cream of mushroom soup, undiluted
1/2 cup grated sharp Cheddar cheese

1 egg, well beaten
1/2 cup mayonnaise
1 Tablespoon grated onion
1/2 cup cheese cracker crumbs

Preheat oven to 400°F. Cook broccoli 5 minutes. Drain well. Combine soup, cheese, egg, mayonnaise, and onion in medium-size mixing bowl; add broccoli and stir to combine. Pour into a 1-quart casserole. Sprinkle with cracker crumbs and bake 25 to 30 minutes, or until browned on top.   *6 servings*

Nice to know: This recipe can be assembled in the morning and kept in the refrigerator ready to go into the oven just before company arrives.

CORN PUDDING

An old-time favorite.

1 Tablespoon butter or
   margarine, melted
3 eggs, well-beaten
1 can (17 ounces)
   Stokely's Finest®
   Whole Kernel Golden
   Corn, drained
1 can (17 ounces)
   Stokely's Finest®
   Cream Style Golden
   Corn

2 Tablespoons all-purpose
   flour
1 cup milk
1 teaspoon sugar
1/2 teaspoon salt
   Dash pepper

Preheat oven to 350°F. Combine all ingredients. Pour into greased 1 1/2-quart casserole. Place casserole in pan of water. Bake, uncovered, 1 hour and 20 minutes, or until knife inserted in center comes out clean.   *6 servings*

Microwave Method: Combine all ingredients. Pour into greased 2-quart casserole. Microcook uncovered, 20 minutes, or until center is almost set. Rotate dish every 5 minutes. Remove from oven and let stand 3 minutes to finish cooking.

CHINESE GREEN BEAN CASSEROLE

A touch of the Orient.

2 cans (16 ounces each)
   Stokely's Finest®
   Sliced French Style
   Green Beans, drained
1 can (16 ounces) bean
   sprouts, drained

1 can (10 3/4 ounces)
   condensed cream of
   celery soup, undiluted
1 can (3 ounces)
   French-fried onion
   rings

Preheat oven to 350°F. Mix green beans, bean sprouts, and soup in greased 2-quart casserole. Bake 30 minutes. Sprinkle with onion rings and bake an additional 5 minutes, or until onion rings are golden brown.   *10 to 12 servings*

CARROT CASSEROLE

Substitute cream of chicken soup for variety.

2 cans (16 ounces each)
   Stokely's Finest®
   Sliced Carrots
   well drained
1 can (10 3/4 ounces)
   condensed cream of
   celery soup,
   undiluted

1 cup grated American
   cheese
1/2 cup dry bread crumbs
2 Tablespoons butter or
   margarine, melted

Preheat oven to 350°F. Combine carrots, soup, and cheese in 1 1/2-quart casserole. Mix bread crumbs and butter together; sprinkle over top of casserole. Bake 25 to 30 minutes.   *8 servings*

SOUR CREAM FRIJOLES

A Mexican favorite.

1 can (15 1/2 ounces)
   Van Camp's® Mexican
   Style Chili Beans
1/2 cup commercial sour
   cream

1/2 cup grated American
   cheese
1/4 cup chopped scallion
   (green onion),
   including tops

Heat beans in saucepan. Stir in sour cream and cook over moderate heat just until heated through. Pour into serving bowl and garnish with cheese and scallion.   *4 servings*

BAYOU PAN DINNER

Ideal for a hurried schedule.

1 can (15 ounces)
   Van Camp's® New
   Orleans Style Red
   Kidney Beans
3 slices bacon

1/4 cup chopped onion
1 can (15 ounces)
   Van Camp's® Spanish
   Rice
1/4 teaspoon salt

Drain beans. Cook bacon until crisp. Drain bacon on paper towel, reserving 2 Tablespoons drippings in skillet. Sauté onion in drippings until transparent. Add beans, Spanish rice, and salt; heat through. Garnish with crumbled bacon.   *5 servings*

CREOLE SKILLET

A delightful and filling combination.

2 Tablespoons butter or margarine	1 can (17 ounces) Stokely's Finest® Whole Kernel Golden Corn, drained
1/4 cup chopped onion	
1 can (15 ounces) Van Camp's® New Orleans Style Red Kidney Beans, drained	1 can (15 ounces) Van Camp's® Spanish Rice
1 can (16 ounces) Stokely's Finest® Cut Green Beans, drained	1/4 teaspoon salt Onion rings or 2 cups crushed potato chips (optional)

Melt butter in skillet; sauté onion until transparent. Add kidney beans, green beans, corn, Spanish rice, and salt. Mix well and cook until heated through. Transfer to serving dish and garnish with onion rings or crushed potato chips if desired.   *6 servings*

Microwave Method: Melt butter in 2 1/2-quart casserole in microwave oven. Add onion and microcook 2 minutes, or until transparent. Add kidney beans, green beans, corn, Spanish rice, and salt. Cover and microcook 4 minutes, or until heated through. Stir after 2 minutes. Transfer to serving dish and garnish with onion rings or crushed potato chips if desired.

HAWAIIAN PORK 'N BEANS

Beans with a pleasant sweet touch.

1 can (31 ounces) Van Camp's® Pork and Beans	1/2 teaspoon ginger
1/3 cup firmly packed brown sugar	3 or 4 pineapple slices

Preheat oven to 350°F. Combine beans, sugar, and ginger in a 1-quart casserole. Arrange pineapple slices attractively on top and nestle into beans. Bake, uncovered, 40 to 45 minutes.   *6 servings*

Opposite: Creole Skillet

A RECIPE FOR Creole Skillet
tablespoons butter
margarine

SAUERKRAUT-NOODLE BAKE

Serve with German sausage for a hearty meal.

4 ounces (about 3 cups)
fine noodles
1/4 cup butter or margarine
1 can (16 ounces)
Stokely's Finest®
Bavarian Style
Sauerkraut, rinsed
and drained

1 cup grated sharp Cheddar
cheese
Salt to taste

Preheat oven to 350°F. Cook noodles according to package directions; drain and stir in butter. Layer half each sauerkraut, noodles, and cheese in 2-quart casserole. Sprinkle with salt. Repeat layer. Cover and bake 30 minutes.   *5 servings*

DEEP-FRIED VEGETABLE MEDLEY

Serve as a side dish or as an hors d'oeuvre.

4 cups vegetable oil
1 package (10 ounces)
Frozen Stokely's®
Brussels Sprouts
1 package (10 ounces)
Frozen Stokely's®
Cauliflower
1 package (10 ounces)
Frozen Stokely's®
Broccoli Spears

1 egg, well beaten
1/2 cup toasted wheat germ
or matzo meal
1/2 cup seasoned bread
crumbs
1/2 to 3/4 cup all-purpose
flour
1 to 2 teaspoons salt
Pepper to taste

Preheat oil to 375°F. Place vegetables in shallow baking dish and cover with boiling water. Let stand 2 to 3 minutes; drain. To remove excess moisture, place vegetables on paper towels. Cut broccoli spears in half crosswise. Place beaten egg in small bowl. Combine wheat germ, bread crumbs, flour, salt, and pepper in heavy plastic bag; shake to blend flavors. Dip each vegetable piece in egg, turning to coat evenly. Place several vegetable pieces in plastic bag; shake to coat well. Repeat process. Place coated vegetables in hot oil; deep fry until golden brown. Drain on paper towels and keep warm. Serve with lemon wedges.   *6 servings*

CREAMED SPINACH RING

One of Mrs. Alfred Stokely's favorites.

2 packages (10 ounces each) Frozen Stokely's® Chopped Spinach
2 Tablespoons butter or margarine
2 Tablespoons chopped onion
2 Tablespoons all-purpose flour
2 eggs, separated
2 cans (10 3/4 ounces each) condensed cream of mushroom soup, undiluted, divided
1/3 cup half-and-half
1/2 teaspoon nutmeg
Salt and pepper to taste
1 hard-cooked egg
1 jar (2 ounces) Stokely's Finest® Sliced Pimientos, drained

Preheat oven to 325°F. Grease a 4-cup ring mold. Cook spinach according to package directions; drain and squeeze excess moisture from spinach. Melt butter, add onion, and sauté until transparent. Stir in flour and beaten egg yolks, 1/3 cup undiluted soup, and the half-and-half, stirring constantly. Add spinach, nutmeg, salt, and pepper. Cook, stirring occasionally, until thickened. Cool. Meanwhile, beat egg whites until stiff peaks form; carefully fold into cooled spinach mixture. Turn into ring mold and set mold in pan of hot water. Bake 50 minutes, or until set. Carefully invert spinach ring onto heated platter. Warm remaining undiluted soup and fill center of ring mold with heated soup. Garnish soup with chopped hard-cooked egg. Garnish spinach ring with pimientos.   *6 servings*

EASTERN BEANS

Beans with a Boston accent.

1 can (16 ounces) Van Camp's® Pork and Beans
1 teaspoon instant minced onion
1 Tablespoon molasses
1 teaspoon prepared mustard
1/2 teaspoon prepared horseradish

Combine all ingredients in medium-size saucepan and simmer 15 minutes. Serve immediately.   *4 servings*

Variation: Top these beans with pork chops fixed your favorite way.

MILANO MEDLEY

A vegetarian's treat.

1 package (16 ounces)
  Frozen Stokely's®
  Vegetables Milano®
1 cup water, divided
2 Tablespoons vegetable
  oil
4 teaspoons cornstarch
1 Tablespoon sugar
1 Tablespoon instant
  minced onion

3/4 teaspoon salt
1/2 teaspoon garlic salt
  Dash pepper
1/4 cup white vinegar
2 medium-size tomatoes,
  quartered
1/4 cup walnut pieces
  Spaghetti noodles,
  cooked

Cook vegetables in 1/2 cup water 8 to 9 minutes; drain and set aside. Combine 1/2 cup water, oil, cornstarch, sugar, onion, salt, garlic salt, pepper, and vinegar in medium-size skillet. Cook, stirring constantly, until thickened. Add reserved vegetables, tomatoes, and walnuts; stir until coated with sauce. Cover and cook until heated through, 1 to 2 minutes. Serve over spaghetti noodles.   *6 servings*

VEGETABLES DEL SOL
IN GOLDEN PUFF

The cheese flavor adds zest.

1/2 of 16-ounce package
  (8 ounces)
  Frozen Stokely's®
  Vegetables del Sol®
2 eggs, separated
1/2 teaspoon sugar

1/8 teaspoon cayenne
1 teaspoon salt
1 can (10 3/4 ounces)
  condensed Cheddar cheese
  soup, undiluted
  Paprika

Preheat oven to 350°F. Prepare vegetables according to package directions; drain. Place in shallow, buttered baking dish. Beat egg yolks with sugar, cayenne, and salt; add to cheese soup. Beat egg whites and fold into cheese sauce. Pour over vegetables. Sprinkle with paprika. Bake 40 minutes, or until sauce is firm.
4 to 6 servings

Opposite: Gatorade® thirst quencher, Milano Medley

MOM'S BAKED BEANS

An all-time favorite.

1 Tablespoon chopped
onion
1 Tablespoon butter or
margarine
1 can (21 ounces)
Van Camp's® Pork
and Beans

1/4 cup firmly packed brown
sugar
2 Tablespoons Stokely's
Finest® Tomato Catsup

Preheat oven to 350°F. Sauté onion in butter until transparent. Combine onion with remaining ingredients in greased 1 1/2-quart casserole. Bake, uncovered, 1 hour and 10 minutes.   *4 servings*

SPANISH CORN AND ZUCCHINI

A new way to cook zucchini.

3 Tablespoons butter or
margarine
1/2 cup chopped onion
1/2 cup chopped green
pepper
1 clove garlic, minced
1 pound zucchini,
unpeeled, thinly
sliced
1 can (17 ounces)
Stokely's Finest®
Whole Kernel Golden
Corn, drained

1 can (8 ounces)
Stokely's Finest®
Tomato Sauce
1 teaspoon Worcestershire
sauce
1 teaspoon sugar
1/2 teaspoon salt
1/2 teaspoon chili powder
1/8 teaspoon dry mustard
Dash pepper

Melt butter in large skillet. Sauté onion, green pepper, and garlic until onion is transparent. Add zucchini and cook 10 minutes over low heat. Add remaining ingredients and cook 20 minutes, stirring occasionally and being careful not to break zucchini slices.
6 servings

Microwave Method: Place butter in 2 1/2-quart casserole. Microcook, covered, 1 minute. Add onion, green pepper, and garlic; microcook, covered, 3 minutes, or until onion is transparent. Add zucchini, cover, and microcook 8 minutes, stirring gently twice. Add remaining ingredients, cover, and microcook 5 minutes, stirring once.

SAUCY BEETS

Beets with character.

2 Tablespoons butter or
   margarine, melted
2 Tablespoons cornstarch
1 can (16 ounces)
   Stokely's Finest®
   Sliced Beets

2 Tablespoons brown sugar
2 teaspoons prepared
   horseradish
1/8 teaspoon salt

Blend butter and cornstarch in saucepan. Drain beets, reserving 3/4 cup liquid. Stir reserved liquid, brown sugar, horseradish, and salt into cornstarch mixture and cook until mixture begins to thicken, stirring constantly. Add beets and heat to serving temperature.   *4 servings*

Microwave Method: Place butter in 1-quart casserole. Microcook, covered, 30 seconds, or until melted. Blend in cornstarch. Drain beets, reserving 3/4 cup liquid. Stir reserved beet liquid, brown sugar, horseradish, and salt into first mixture. Microcook 2 minutes, or until mixture thickens and boils, stirring 3 times. Add beets and microcook, covered, 2 minutes, or until beets are warm, stirring twice.

GREEN BEAN AND
SMOKED CHEESE COMBO

Green beans with a flair.

2 cans (16 ounces each)
   Stokely's Finest®
   Cut Green Beans
1 Tablespoon butter or
   margarine
1 Tablespoon all-purpose
   flour

1/2 cup milk
   Salt and pepper to
   taste
1/2 cup smoked cheese
   spread

Heat beans in their own liquid. In separate pan, melt butter; add flour and stir to make smooth paste. Add milk slowly, stirring constantly until sauce is slightly thickened. Season with salt and pepper. Add cheese, stirring constantly, and cook over low heat until smooth. Drain beans and place in serving dish. Top with sauce.
6 to 8 servings

NUTTY ACORN BEANS

A filling winter dish.

2 acorn squash
1 can (16 ounces)
   Van Camp's® Pork
   and Beans
1/3 cup chopped apples

1/4 cup chopped walnuts
   (optional)
1/4 teaspoon salt
1 Tablespoon brown sugar
   Dash cinnamon

Preheat oven to 400°F. Cut squash in half, lengthwise. Remove seeds and place in ungreased baking dish, cut side down. Pour water around squash to a depth of 1/2 inch. Bake 30 to 40 minutes, or until squash is tender. Meanwhile, combine remaining ingredients in saucepan and warm thoroughly. Remove squash from oven and place on serving platter. Spoon bean mixture into squash and serve immediately.   *4 servings*

CONFETTI BEANS PARMESAN

Crumb topped and delicious.

2 Tablespoons chopped
   celery
2 Tablespoons chopped
   onion
4 Tablespoons butter or
   margarine, melted,
   divided
1 can (15 1/2 ounces)
   Stokely's Finest®
   Sliced French Style
   Wax Beans, drained

2 Tablespoons chopped
   Stokely's Finest®
   Whole Pimientos
2 Tablespoons Parmesan
   cheese
2 Tablespoons dry bread
   crumbs

Sauté celery and onion in 2 Tablespoons butter until tender. Stir in wax beans and pimiento; heat to serving temperature. Place in serving bowl. Combine remaining 2 Tablespoons butter, Parmesan cheese, and bread crumbs; sprinkle over beans.   *4 servings*

Opposite: Nutty Acorn Beans

FRUITY BEAN BAKE

A new sweet treat.

1 can (21 ounces)
Van Camp's® Vegetarian
Style Beans in
Tomato Sauce
1/4 cup firmly packed brown
sugar
1 Tablespoon finely
chopped onion

1/2 teaspoon dry mustard
1 can (13 1/4 ounces)
pineapple chunks,
well drained
1 cup shredded Cheddar
cheese

Preheat oven to 350°F. Combine beans, brown sugar, onion, and mustard in greased 1 1/2-quart casserole. Arrange pineapple chunks on top of beans. Bake 30 minutes. Sprinkle top with cheese; return to oven until cheese melts.   *4 servings*

ELEGANT WAX BEANS PARMESAN

A company dish.

2 Tablespoons chopped
celery
2 Tablespoons chopped
onion
3 Tablespoons butter or
margarine, divided
2 Tablespoons all-purpose
flour
1 can (15 1/2 ounces)
Stokely's Finest®
Sliced French Style
Wax Beans, drained,
liquid reserved

1/4 cup milk
2 Tablespoons dry white
wine
2 Tablespoons Parmesan
cheese
1/4 cup dry bread crumbs
2 Tablespoons chopped
Stokely's Finest®
Pimientos (optional)

In saucepan, sauté celery and onion in 2 Tablespoons butter. Remove from heat and blend in flour. Drain beans, reserving 1/4 cup liquid. Add reserved liquid, milk, and wine. Return to heat and stir until thickened and bubbly; add cheese. Stir in beans and heat to serving temperature. Meanwhile toss bread crumbs with remaining 1 Tablespoon melted butter. Sauté until light brown. Place beans in serving dish and garnish with bread crumbs and pimientos.
4 servings

SWEET 'N SOUR CANTONESE

Try your chopsticks on this.

2 cans (8 ounces each) crushed pineapple	1/4 cup white wine vinegar
1/2 cup sugar	1/4 cup water
2 Tablespoons cornstarch	1 package (14 ounces) Frozen Stokely's® Cantonese Style Stir-Fry Vegetables
1/4 teaspoon ginger	Chow mein noodles
3 Tablespoons vegetable oil, divided	Soy sauce (optional)
1 Tablespoon lemon juice	

Drain pineapple, reserving juice; set both aside. Combine sugar, cornstarch, ginger, 2 Tablespoons oil, lemon juice, 1/4 cup reserved pineapple juice, vinegar, and water, blending until smooth; set sauce aside. Remove seasoning packet from vegetables and add to sauce. Heat 9- or 10-inch covered skillet or wok over high heat until very hot (a drop of water will sizzle). Spread frozen vegetables evenly in hot skillet. Pour remaining Tablespoon oil in wide, circular motion inside rim of pan; stir quickly into vegetables, coating each piece. Add 2 Tablespoons sauce, blending quickly. Cover and cook 2 minutes, stirring once midway. If vegetables begin to stick, reduce temperature slightly or add an additional teaspoon oil. Add remaining sauce to skillet, stir constantly and cook 1 minute. Add pineapple, stirring to blend; cook about 30 seconds. Serve over chow mein noodles. Soy sauce may be added if desired.   *4 servings*

DEVILISH BRUSSELS SPROUTS

Sprouts with pizzazz.

1 package (10 ounces) Frozen Stokely's® Brussels Sprouts	2 teaspoons Worcestershire sauce
1 Tablespoon prepared mustard	1 teaspoon soy sauce
	1/2 teaspoon salt
	Dash pepper

Cook Brussels sprouts according to package directions. Meanwhile, combine remaining ingredients in a medium-size saucepan and simmer 2 to 3 minutes to heat through. Drain sprouts and place in serving dish. Spoon sauce over sprouts and serve.
4 servings

FROZEN VEGETABLES COOKED IN A PACKET

Cooking frozen vegetables in aluminum foil is a great way to save energy. Vegetables can cook in the oven along with a roast, stew, or casserole. Since there is no pan to wash, clean-up is a breeze, and vegetables retain food value because little or no moisture is added. The suggested temperature for cooking frozen vegetables in foil is 400°F., but you can adjust cooking time when you add your packet to an oven set at a lower temperature. Place vegetables on a large sheet of heavy-duty aluminum foil, add 2 Tablespoons of water, 1 Tablespoon butter or margarine, salt and pepper to taste, and your favorite seasoning. To make a packet: bring long ends of foil together and fold over vegetables, crimp ends to form an airtight packet. We suggest you place the packet in a shallow baking dish in case the foil develops a leak. Most frozen vegetables require 45 minutes to 1 hour cooking time.

Cooking in a packet is also an ideal method to use when you are cooking out of doors. Follow the same instructions, placing the packet on the grill. Be sure the flames do not touch the foil, and be sure the coals are hot and glowing before you start to cook.

MICROWAVE COOKING OF CANNED AND FROZEN VEGETABLES

Many homemakers are returning to work and no longer can prepare time-consuming dishes every day. As a result, more and more people depend on canned and frozen vegetables to help them get dinner ready in a hurry. When canned vegetables are warmed and frozen vegetables are cooked in a microwave oven, they are ready to eat by the time the table is set.

Hints to remember about microwave cooking: • Never use a metal container or aluminum foil in a microwave oven. • Microwave cooking is moist cooking and therefore less liquid should be used than in conventional cooking. • Most dishes should be covered during cooking and stirred at least once. • When you are not certain how long to cook a particular food, cook it for a short period and then check it. Add cooking time if necessary, but remember once food is overcooked there is very little you can do to remedy the situation.

To microcook canned vegetables: Drain half the liquid from the vegetables, place in bowl or casserole, season as desired, cover, and microcook 1 to 2 minutes for an 8-ounce can and 2 to 3 minutes for a 16-ounce can. Stir at least once during cooking.

To microcook frozen vegetables: Place vegetables in shallow, microwave-proof, serving container. Do not add water. Cover and defrost on defrost cycle for about 2 1/2 minutes. Drain excess water, leaving about 2 Tablespoons around vegetables. Cover vegetables and microcook about 4 minutes. Check for tenderness and give a quick stir. Additional cooking time may be necessary, but most important, do not overcook. Remember to allow 3 minutes standing time to finish cooking. Season to taste and serve.

HOW TO COOK CANNED VEGETABLES

Canned vegetables are packed in their cans raw and pressure cooked to perfection in the sealed cans. All that's really needed is to bring them to the proper serving temperature. Here are some tips that can help you serve them at the peak of perfection:

- Wipe can lid with damp cloth. Open can.
- Drain liquid into saucepan. Add onion, bouillon, or other seasonings, if desired.
- Gently boil liquid to reduce by half. Add vegetables; cover and heat to serving temperature.
- Drain vegetables. Serve immediately. (Add your favorite vegetable sauce, if desired.)

HOW TO COOK FROZEN VEGETABLES

Frozen vegetables are partially cooked before being packaged but do need further cooking. They may be prepared on top of the stove or in the oven. While oven preparation takes longer, it's an energy saver if the oven is already in use for the main dish. Tips for good preparation:

- Partially thaw leafy vegetables before cooking (just to separate the leaves). Corn on the cob should also be partially thawed to assure thorough heating. It is not necessary to thaw other vegetables before cooking.
- Bring about 1/2 cup salted water to boiling point.
- Add vegetables, cover tightly, return to boil.
- Reduce heat and cook gently until vegetables are just tender.
- Drain vegetables, season, and serve immediately.

Nice to know: all vegetables are naturally high in fiber (bulk) and nicely low in calories!

DILL SAUCED PEAS

Special party peas with an intriguing sauce.

2 Tablespoons butter or margarine, melted	1/8 teaspoon white pepper
2 teaspoons cornstarch	1 can (17 ounces) Stokely's Finest® Peas
1 teaspoon instant chicken flavored bouillon	1/2 cup commercial sour cream
1/4 teaspoon onion salt	1/2 teaspoon dill

In saucepan, blend butter, cornstarch, bouillon, onion salt, and pepper. Drain peas, reserving 1/4 cup liquid. Add reserved liquid to saucepan and stir until smooth. Cook over moderate heat, stirring constantly, until slightly thickened. Add sour cream and dill. Stir in peas and heat to serving temperature but do not boil.   *4 servings*

Nice to know: You may substitute Stokely's Finest® Cut Green Beans for the peas to obtain a different shape and texture in your menu.

CREOLE-STYLE GREEN BEANS

Bacon and tomato flavor the beans.

4 slices bacon, diced	1/8 teaspoon dry mustard
3/4 cup chopped onion	Dash pepper
1/2 cup chopped green pepper	1 can (16 ounces) Stokely's Finest® Stewed Tomatoes, undrained and chunked
2 Tablespoons all-purpose flour	
2 Tablespoons brown sugar	1 can (16 ounces) Stokely's Finest® Cut Green Beans, drained
1 Tablespoon Worcestershire sauce	
1/2 teaspoon salt	

Cook bacon until crisp; drain bacon on paper towel and set aside, reserving 2 Tablespoons drippings in skillet. Sauté onion and green pepper in drippings until onion is transparent. Blend in flour, sugar, Worcestershire sauce, salt, mustard, and pepper. Add stewed tomatoes and cook, stirring constantly, until mixture thickens and boils. Add beans and heat to serving temperature. Spoon into serving dish and top with reserved bacon.   *6 servings*

FLORENTINE VEGETABLES WITH SHRIMP SAUCE

A delicious easy-to-make treat.

1 package (16 ounces)
  Frozen Stokely's®
  Broccoli Florentine®
1 carton (4 ounces)
  whipped cream cheese
1/4 cup milk

1 can (10 3/4 ounces)
  condensed cream of
  shrimp soup, undiluted
2 teaspoons lemon juice
  Toasted slivered almonds

Prepare vegetables according to package directions; drain. Blend cream cheese, milk, and soup in saucepan. Stir until mixture is smooth and heated through. Remove from heat, add lemon juice and stir. Place vegetables in serving dish, pour desired amount of sauce over vegetables, and garnish with almonds. Remaining sauce may be used next day as a creamed soup by diluting with milk.   *6 servings*

THREE BEAN BAKE

A real bean treat!

1/2 cup chopped onion
1 Tablespoon butter or
  margarine
1 can (16 ounces)
  Van Camp's® Pork
  and Beans
1 can (16 ounces)
  Stokely's Finest®
  Lima Beans, drained
1 can (15 ounces)
  Stokely's Finest®
  Dark Red Kidney
  Beans

1/2 cup Stokely's Finest®
  Tomato Catsup
2 Tablespoons brown sugar
1 1/2 teaspoons vinegar
1 teaspoon dry mustard
1 teaspoon salt
3 strips bacon, diced

Preheat oven to 350°F. Sauté onion in butter until tender. In 13×9×2-inch pan, stir together remaining ingredients except bacon. Top with bacon and bake, uncovered, 1 hour and 15 minutes.
8 servings

NEW ENGLAND LIMA BEAN BAKE

Delicious with ham.

2 slices bacon
1 medium-size onion, chopped
1 can (16 ounces) Stokely's Finest® Lima Beans, drained
1/4 cup maple syrup

1/4 cup Stokely's Finest® Tomato Catsup
1 teaspoon Worcestershire sauce
1/2 teaspoon salt
Pepper to taste

Preheat oven to 350°F. Cook bacon until crisp. Drain bacon on paper towel. In bacon drippings, sauté onion until transparent. Meanwhile combine lima beans, maple syrup, catsup, Worcestershire sauce, salt, and pepper in 1-quart casserole. Crumble bacon and stir into lima beans along with onion and drippings. Cover and bake 20 to 25 minutes.   *4 servings*

Microwave Method: Dice bacon and microcook in 1 1/2-quart covered casserole until bacon is crisp. Add onion, lima beans, maple syrup, catsup, Worcestershire sauce, salt, and pepper. Stir to blend. Cover and microcook 5 minutes, stirring after 2 1/2 minutes.

PEAS À LA CRÈME

A hint of France in this side dish.

1/3 cup commercial sour cream
1/2 teaspoon instant chicken flavored bouillon
1/2 teaspoon lemon juice

Dash pepper
1 can (16 ounces) Stokely's Finest® Peas
Fresh dill (optional)

Mix sour cream and bouillon in saucepan. Let stand 10 minutes to dissolve bouillon. Add lemon juice and pepper. Place over low heat to blend flavors; do not boil. Heat peas in their own liquid; drain. Place in serving dish; top with sauce, and garnish with fresh dill if desired.   *4 servings*

Opposite: Hominy Olé (page 113), Glazed Carrots (page 112), Peas à la Crème, Honeyed Beets (page 112), New England Lima Bean Bake

GLAZED CARROTS

This side dish will bring you compliments.

2 Tablespoons brown sugar
2 Tablespoons butter or
  margarine
  Salt to taste
1/8 teaspoon pumpkin pie
  spice

1 can (16 ounces)
  Stokely's Finest®
  Sliced Carrots, drained

Combine brown sugar, butter, salt, and spice in large skillet. Add carrots and cook over moderate heat until carrots are hot and glazed, stirring occasionally.   *4 servings*

HONEYED BEETS

A honey of a dish.

2 Tablespoons butter or
  margarine, melted
1 teaspoon cornstarch
3 Tablespoons honey
2 Tablespoons water
1 teaspoon lemon juice

Dash salt
1 can (16 ounces)
  Stokely's Finest®
  Tiny Whole Beets,
  drained

Melt butter in saucepan; blend in cornstarch. Stir in honey, water, lemon juice, and salt. Cook over medium heat, stirring constantly, until mixture thickens and comes to a boil. Add beets, turning to coat. Cover and cook just until heated through.
4 servings

SWEET PEAS AND CARROTS

An easy way to dress up plain vegetables.

1 package (10 ounces)
  Frozen Stokely's® Peas
  and Carrots

2 Tablespoons apple jelly
1 teaspoon lemon juice

Cook peas and carrots according to package directions. Drain. Add apple jelly and lemon juice. Stir to dissolve jelly. Serve at once.   *4 servings*

HOMINY OLÉ

A spicy and delicious one-dish meal.

1/2 pound bacon, diced
1 cup chopped onion
1 can (20 ounces)
  Van Camp's® Golden
  Hominy, drained
1 can (16 ounces)
  Stokely's Finest®
  Stewed Tomatoes

1 package (1 1/4 ounces)
  taco seasoning mix
2 cups grated American
  cheese
Hot pepper sauce

In large skillet, cook bacon and onion. Drain all but 2 Tablespoons drippings from skillet. Add hominy and sauté 5 minutes. Blend in tomatoes, seasoning mix, cheese, and hot pepper sauce. Heat thoroughly, stirring until cheese is melted.   *6 servings*

PEAS WITH MAPLE SYRUP

A hint of New England.

1 Tablespoon butter or
  margarine
2 Tablespoons maple syrup

1 can (17 ounces)
  Stokely's Finest®
  Peas, drained

Heat butter and syrup in saucepan. Stir in peas; heat to serving temperature.   *3 servings*

ORANGE GLAZED BEETS

Just great.

1 can (16 ounces)
  Stokely's Finest®
  Cut Beets
1 Tablespoon butter or
  margarine

2 teaspoons all-purpose
  flour
2 Tablespoons brown sugar
1/2 cup orange juice
  Orange peel

Heat beets in their own liquid. In separate saucepan, melt butter. Remove from heat; stir in flour until smooth. Add brown sugar and orange juice. Return to heat, stirring constantly, until thickened. Drain beets and add to sauce mixture. Garnish with orange peel.   *4 to 5 servings*

FAVORITE LIMA BARBECUE

Great for picnic take-along.

1 package (10 ounces)
   Frozen Stokely's®
   Fordhook Lima Beans
1/4 cup diced onion
   Dash garlic powder
2 Tablespoons vegetable
   oil
1 can (8 ounces)
   Stokely's Finest®
   Tomato Sauce

3 Tablespoons brown sugar
1 1/2 Tablespoons lemon juice
1/2 teaspoon dry mustard
3/4 teaspoon salt
2 teaspoons
   Worcestershire sauce

Cook lima beans according to package directions; drain. Meanwhile, sauté onion and garlic powder in oil until onion is tender. Stir in tomato sauce, brown sugar, lemon juice, mustard, salt, and Worcestershire. Heat to boiling. Reduce heat and simmer, uncovered, 15 minutes. Add drained beans and simmer an additional 10 minutes, or until sauce is slightly thickened.   *4 servings*

CHEESY CAULIFLOWER AND PEAS

A great dish to serve with ham.

1 package (10 ounces)
   Frozen Stokely's®
   Cauliflower
1 package (9 ounces)
   Frozen Stokely's®
   Green Peas
1 Tablespoon butter or
   margarine
1 Tablespoon all-purpose
   flour

1/2 cup milk
1/2 cup grated American
   cheese
1 1/2 teaspoons Worcestershire
   sauce
   Cayenne to taste
1 jar (2 ounces)
   Stokely's Finest®
   Sliced Pimientos,
   drained

Cook cauliflower and peas according to package directions, drain, and set aside. Melt butter in medium-size saucepan, add flour, and stir briskly. Add milk and heat, stirring constantly until thickened and bubbly. Remove from heat, stir in cheese, Worcestershire, and cayenne, stirring constantly until cheese is melted. Return pan to low heat, add reserved vegetables, and cook 2 minutes. Spoon into serving bowl and garnish with pimientos.   *6 servings*

CRANBERRY BEETS

Delicious with turkey or ham.

1 can (16 ounces)
  Stokely's Finest®
  Diced Beets, drained
1 can (16 ounces) whole
  berry or jellied
  cranberry sauce

2 Tablespoons orange
  juice
1 teaspoon grated orange
  rind
  Dash salt

Combine all ingredients in saucepan. Heat thoroughly, stirring occasionally. Serve at once.   *6 servings*

MAMA'S SOUTHERN GREEN BEANS

A slow-cook method.

1 can (16 ounces)
  Stokely's Finest®
  Cut Green Beans
1 medium-size onion,
  sliced

3 slices bacon
  Salt and pepper to
  taste

In saucepan, place green beans, onion, bacon, and seasoning. Cover and simmer 1 hour. Serve with slotted spoon.   *4 servings*

Nice to know: Ingredients may be cooked in slow cooker 4 hours on the low setting.

SPROUTS AMANDINE

A delightful way to cook Brussels sprouts.

1 package (10 ounces)
  Frozen Stokely's®
  Brussels Sprouts
3 Tablespoons butter or
  margarine

1/4 cup slivered almonds
1/2 teaspoon tarragon
1 Tablespoon lemon juice

Prepare Brussels sprouts according to package directions; drain and keep warm. Melt butter in medium-size skillet; sauté almonds until lightly browned; add tarragon and stir. Sprinkle lemon juice over Brussels sprouts; add sprouts to skillet, and toss lightly. Sauté briefly to reheat. Transfer to serving dish.   *4 servings*

PIQUANT VEGETABLE COMBO

A refreshing textured dish.

1 package (10 ounces) Frozen Stokely's® Broccoli Spears	1/2 cup bread crumbs 2 Tablespoons butter or margarine
1 package (10 ounces) Frozen Stokely's® Cauliflower	4 slices bacon 1 clove garlic, minced 1/4 cup cider vinegar

Cook broccoli and cauliflower together until both are tender. Brown bread crumbs in butter and set aside. Meanwhile cook bacon in skillet until crisp. Remove bacon and drain on paper towel; add garlic, and sauté lightly; add vinegar. Drain vegetables well and place in serving dish. Pour sauce evenly over vegetables. Top with bread crumbs and crumbled bacon.   *6 servings*

SPINACH-ZUCCHINI BOATS

An elegant stuffed vegetable, guaranteed to please everyone.

3 medium-size zucchini (about 1 1/2 pounds) Salt	1 can (4 1/2 ounces) sliced mushrooms, drained
2 Tablespoons butter or margarine	1/4 teaspoon nutmeg 1/2 cup grated Parmesan cheese
3 Tablespoons all-purpose flour	
1 cup milk	
1 package (10 ounces) Frozen Stokely's® Chopped Spinach, cooked and well drained	

Preheat oven to 350°F. Trim ends from zucchini and cook in salted boiling water 10 to 12 minutes; drain thoroughly. Split zucchini in half lengthwise, scoop out flesh to within 1/2 inch of side to form boats, reserving flesh and setting shells aside. Chop flesh and set aside. Melt butter in medium-size saucepan, add flour and stir briskly. Add milk and cook until thickened, stirring constantly. Add reserved chopped zucchini, spinach, mushrooms, and nutmeg and stir until well combined. Remove from heat. Place zucchini boats in shallow baking dish and fill with spinach mixture. Sprinkle with grated cheese and bake 15 to 20 minutes, or until cheese melts and zucchini is tender.   *6 servings*

ASPARAGUS WITH GOLDEN FRUIT SAUCE

Asparagus with a sassy flair.

1 can (14 1/2 ounces)
    Stokely's Finest® Cut
    Asparagus Spears, or
    1 package (8 ounces)
    Frozen Stokely's®
    Asparagus Spears
2 Tablespoons butter or
    margarine

2 egg yolks, beaten
1/8 teaspoon salt
5 Tablespoons orange
    juice
1 teaspoon lemon juice

Warm canned asparagus or cook frozen asparagus according to package directions. Meanwhile, melt butter in small saucepan. Carefully blend in beaten egg yolks, salt, orange juice, and lemon juice. Cook and stir over low heat until thick and smooth. Drain asparagus and top with sauce.   *4 servings*

RAISIN-PINEAPPLE BEETS

A nice flavor combination.

1/4 cup butter or margarine,
    melted
2 Tablespoons cornstarch
1/4 teaspoon salt
1 can (16 ounces)
    Stokely's Finest®
    Tiny Whole Beets

1 can (13 1/2 ounces)
    pineapple chunks
1/4 cup firmly packed brown
    sugar
1/3 cup raisins

Blend butter, cornstarch, and salt in medium-size saucepan. Drain beets reserving 1/2 cup liquid; drain pineapple reserving all liquid. Stir reserved liquids and brown sugar into butter mixture. Cook over medium heat, stirring constantly until mixture thickens and becomes clear. Add beets, pineapple, and raisins; simmer about 5 minutes.   *6 servings*

SWISS BEANS

Beans with class!

2 Tablespoons butter or
  margarine, divided
1 Tablespoon all-purpose
  flour
1/4 teaspoon salt
  Dash pepper
1/2 teaspoon instant
  minced onion
1/2 cup commercial sour
  cream

1 can (16 ounces)
  Stokely's Finest®
  Sliced French Style
  Green Beans, drained
1 cup grated process
  Swiss cheese (about
  1/4 pound)
1 cup crushed cornflakes

Preheat oven to 350°F. Melt 1 Tablespoon butter in saucepan, add flour, salt, pepper, onion, and sour cream. Gently stir in green beans and place in a 1-quart casserole. Cover with grated cheese. Mix 1 Tablespoon melted butter and the cornflakes. Sprinkle over grated cheese. Bake, uncovered, 20 minutes. *6 servings*

HOT MILANO SALAD

Hot and delightful.

1 package (16 ounces)
  Frozen Stokely's®
  Vegetables Milano®
8 strips bacon
1/2 cup chopped onion
2 Tablespoons all-purpose
  flour
2 Tablespoons sugar

1 1/2 teaspoons salt
1 teaspoon celery seed
  Pepper to taste
1/3 cup cider vinegar
1 cup water
2 hard-cooked eggs,
  chopped

Cook vegetables according to package directions; drain. Cook bacon until crisp; crumble and set aside, reserving 2 Tablespoons drippings in skillet. Sauté onion in drippings until transparent. Stir in flour, sugar, salt, celery seed, and pepper. Add vinegar and water; stir over moderate heat until thick and bubbly. Stir in vegetables and eggs. Heat through and serve garnished with reserved bacon.
8 servings

ORANGED PARISIAN VEGETABLES

A new way to add variety to your diet.

3 Tablespoons butter or
   margarine
1/2 cup orange juice
   Salt to taste
1 package (16 ounces)
   Frozen Stokely's®
   Vegetables Parisian™

1/3 cup sliced black olives
1 Tablespoon chopped
   parsley

Melt butter in medium-size saucepan. Add orange juice and salt. Bring mixture to a boil. Add vegetables, lower heat, cover, and cook until vegetables are just tender. Remove from heat, stir in olives, place in serving bowl, and sprinkle with parsley. Serve immediately.   *6 servings*

Nice to know: Sauce may be thickened with 1 teaspoon cornstarch.

SAVORY LIMA BEANS

Serve with cornbread.

2 slices bacon
1 Tablespoon all-purpose
   flour
1/2 teaspoon sugar
1 can (16 ounces)
   Stokely's Finest®
   Stewed Tomatoes

1 can (16 ounces)
   Stokely's Finest®
   Fordhook Green Lima
   Beans, drained
   Salt to taste

Cook bacon until crisp. Drain bacon on paper towel, reserving 2 Tablespoons drippings in skillet. Mix flour and sugar; add to skillet, stirring to blend. Add tomatoes and lima beans. Heat, stirring constantly, until mixture thickens slightly and is heated through. Add salt to taste. Place in serving dish and top with crumbled bacon.   *6 servings*

HOMINY AU GRATIN

A substitute for potatoes.

1 can (29 ounces)
   Van Camp's® White
   Hominy, drained
1/4 cup chopped onion
1/4 cup chopped
   Stokely's Finest®
   Whole Pimientos, drained
2 Tablespoons butter or
   margarine, melted

2 Tablespoons all-purpose
   flour
1 teaspoon salt
1 cup milk
1 cup grated American or
   Cheddar cheese

Preheat oven to 350°F. Combine hominy, onion, and pimientos in greased 1 1/2-quart casserole. In saucepan, blend butter, flour, and salt; stir in milk. Cook, stirring constantly, until mixture bubbles and thickens. Stir in cheese and heat until cheese is melted. Pour over the hominy. Bake 20 minutes.   *4 to 5 servings*

GREEN BEANS WITH BACON DRESSING

Worth the effort.

5 slices bacon
2 eggs, well beaten
1/3 cup cider vinegar
1/2 cup water
3 Tablespoons sugar

1/4 teaspoon salt
2 cans (16 ounces each)
   Stokely's Finest®
   Whole Green Beans

Cook bacon until crisp; drain bacon on paper towel and crumble. Set bacon aside and reserve 1/4 cup drippings in skillet. Beat eggs with vinegar, water, sugar, and salt. Add egg mixture to drippings; cook over low heat, stirring constantly with wire whisk until thickened. Heat beans in saucepan; drain and arrange in serving dish. Pour hot dressing over beans. Sprinkle with crumbled bacon.   *8 servings*

Microwave Method: In casserole microcook bacon 4 minutes, or until crisp. Set bacon aside and reserve 1/4 cup drippings in dish. Beat eggs with vinegar, water, sugar, and salt. Add egg mixture to drippings; microcook, uncovered, 3 to 4 minutes, or until thickened;

beat egg mixture with wire whisk twice during cooking. (Sauce will curdle if not whipped vigorously.) Place beans in casserole, cover, and microcook 2 to 3 minutes, or until hot. Drain and arrange in serving dish; pour hot dressing over beans. Sprinkle with crumbled bacon.

EASY SPINACH

Even kids will eat it!

4 slices bacon
1/4 cup chopped onion
1 can (15 ounces) Stokely's Finest® Spinach, drained, liquid reserved

1 hard-cooked egg, sliced
Cider vinegar (optional)

Cook bacon until crisp; remove bacon and drain on paper towel; reserve 2 Tablespoons drippings in skillet. Sauté onion in drippings until tender. Add liquid drained from spinach to skillet and bring to boil. Simmer 2 to 3 minutes to reduce liquid to half the original amount. Add spinach and heat through. Place in serving dish; top with crumbled bacon and egg slices. Serve with vinegar, if desired.   *4 servings*

GOLDEN HOMINY PARMESAN

As easy as it is delicious.

1 Tablespoon butter or margarine
1/2 medium-size onion cut into rings
1 can (14 1/2 ounces) Van Camp's® Golden Hominy with Red and Green Peppers, drained

1/4 teaspoon seasoned salt
1 Tablespoon Parmesan cheese

Melt butter in 8-inch skillet. Separate onion rings and sauté until transparent. Add hominy and sprinkle with seasoned salt. Heat to serving temperature. Place in serving dish; top with Parmesan cheese.   *3 to 4 servings*

GERMAN-STYLE HOMINY

Delicious with fish.

4 slices bacon, diced	1/4 cup sugar
1/2 cup chopped onion	1/2 teaspoon salt
3 Tablespoons all-purpose flour	1/8 teaspoon pepper
1/2 cup water	1 can (20 ounces) Van Camp's® White Hominy, drained
1/4 cup cider vinegar	

Cook bacon until crisp; set aside. Drain drippings reserving 3 Tablespoons in skillet. Sauté onion in reserved drippings. Blend in flour. Stir in water and vinegar. Cook until thick and bubbly. Add sugar, salt, and pepper. Fold in hominy and cooked bacon; heat to serving temperature.   *4 servings*

SAUCED WAX BEANS

A bean dish with variety.

1 can (10 3/4 ounces) condensed Cheddar cheese soup, undiluted	1 jar (2 ounces) Stokely's Finest® Sliced Pimientos, drained
2 cans (15 1/2 ounces each) Stokely's Finest® Cut Wax Beans, drained	1/2 cup seasoned bread crumbs
1 can (16 ounces) small whole white onions, drained	1 Tablespoon butter or margarine

Heat cheese soup in 2-quart saucepan until warmed through. Add beans and onions to soup along with pimientos and heat to serving temperature. In small skillet, sauté bread crumbs in butter until lightly browned. Place cheese-vegetable mixture in serving dish. Garnish with bread crumbs.   *8 servings*

BRUSSELS SPROUTS ROYAL

An attractive side dish.

1 package (10 ounces)
Frozen Stokely's®
Brussels Sprouts
2 Tablespoons butter or
margarine
1/4 cup fine dry bread
crumbs

1 hard-cooked egg yolk,
sieved
2 teaspoons snipped
parsley

Cook sprouts according to package directions; drain. Meanwhile, melt butter in small saucepan until it begins to brown; add crumbs, egg yolk, and parsley. Spoon mixture over hot sprouts; toss lightly and serve. *4 servings*

SAUERKRAUT BAKE

A low-calorie dish.

1 can (16 ounces)
Stokely's Finest®
Shredded Sauerkraut,
well drained

2 medium-size apples,
cored and sliced
1 teaspoon granulated
sugar substitute

Preheat oven to 350°F. Combine all ingredients in 1-quart casserole. Cover and bake 30 minutes. *4 servings*

GOLDENROD GREEN BEANS

Attractive and tasty for a pitch-in dinner.

1 can (16 ounces)
Stokely's Finest®
Cut Green Beans
1 1/2 teaspoons butter or
margarine
1 1/2 teaspoons all-purpose
flour

1/8 teaspoon salt
Dash pepper
1/4 cup milk
1 hard-cooked egg
1/4 cup mayonnaise-type
salad dressing

Heat beans in their own liquid. Meanwhile, in a small saucepan, melt butter, blend in flour, salt, and pepper. Add milk; cook, stirring constantly until mixture thickens. Remove from heat. Chop egg white and stir with salad dressing into sauce. Drain beans; place in serving dish. Top with sauce and sprinkle with egg yolk that has been pressed through a sieve. *4 servings*

SWEET-SOUR SHELLIE BEANS

A favorite from farm days.

2 slices bacon	1 Tablespoon sugar
1/3 cup chopped onion	1/8 teaspoon salt
1 can (16 ounces) Stokely's Finest® Shellie® Beans, drained, liquid reserved	Dash pepper
	2 Tablespoons white vinegar

Cook bacon until crisp. Crumble and set aside. Sauté onion in drippings until transparent. Add liquid drained from beans. Cook liquid down to about 1/2 cup. Add remaining ingredients; gently fold in beans. Heat to serving temperature. Garnish with crumbled bacon.   *4 servings*

ORANGE SHELL SQUASH

You'll make a good impression with this recipe.

1 package (12 ounces) Frozen Stokely's® Cooked Squash	1/2 teaspoon salt
	Pepper to taste
2 Tablespoons brown sugar	2 oranges, halved, pulp removed
2 Tablespoons butter or margarine	4 large marshmallows

Preheat oven to 350°F. Cook squash according to package directions. Add brown sugar, butter, salt, and pepper. Mix well. Place a quarter of mixture in each orange shell. Bake 15 minutes. Place marshmallow on top and heat until melted.   *4 servings*

Salads and Dressings

CORNY-CHICKEN SALAD

A make-ahead salad with spicy flavor.

1 package (16 ounces) Frozen Stokely's® Chuckwagon Corn
2 cups cubed cooked chicken
1/2 head lettuce, shredded
2 cups crushed taco-flavored tortilla chips
1 1/2 cups black olives, divided
1 cup grated American cheese
Tomato wedges
American cheese strips
Whole tortilla chips
Russian dressing or taco sauce

Cook corn according to package directions, drain and chill. Combine corn and chicken. In large salad bowl, layer half of each: lettuce, chips, corn and chicken mixture, 1/4 cup sliced olives, and cheese. Repeat layers. Garnish with tomato wedges, 1 cup whole olives, cheese strips, and whole chips. Serve with Russian dressing or taco sauce.   *6 servings*

VEGETABLE PEPPERONI SALAD

Serve salad with toasted, buttered French bread for a super lunch.

1 package (16 ounces) Frozen Stokely's® Vegetables Milano®
1 medium-size head lettuce, torn
2 tomatoes, cut in wedges (optional)
4 ounces mozzarella cheese, cubed
2 hard-cooked eggs, diced
1/2 cup thinly sliced pepperoni
1/4 cup sliced scallion (green onion)
2 Tablespoons sliced black olives
1/2 cup Italian dressing
Salt and pepper to taste
1 jar (4 ounces) Stokely's Finest® Sliced Pimientos, drained

Cook frozen vegetables according to package directions, drain, and cool. In a large salad bowl, combine all ingredients except dressing, salt, pepper, and pimientos. Toss mixture lightly with dressing, season to taste, and garnish with pimientos.   *8 servings*

UNCOMMON SALAD

An unusual taste combination.

1 can (6 1/2 ounces) tuna, drained and flaked
1 package (10 ounces) Frozen Stokely's® Green Peas, thawed
2 medium-size tomatoes, chopped
1 cup cubed American cheese
1/2 cup diced celery
1/4 cup sweet pickle relish
2 Tablespoons chopped scallion (green onion)
1/4 teaspoon salt
1/8 teaspoon pepper
1/3 cup mayonnaise

Combine all ingredients. Cover and chill 1 hour. Serve on lettuce leaves.   *6 servings*

Opposite: Vegetable Pepperoni Salad

SUPERB FRENCH SALAD DRESSING

Easy — inexpensive — excellent.

1 medium-size onion, quartered	1 1/2 teaspoons salt
1/2 cup white vinegar	1 cup vegetable oil
1/2 cup Stokely's Finest® Tomato Catsup	1 cup sugar

Place onion, vinegar, catsup, and salt in blender; blend until onion is puréed. Gradually add oil and sugar; continue blending until mixture is slightly thickened. Keeps in refrigerator for weeks.
3 cups

NEW ORLEANS BEAN SALAD

A southern treat.

1 can (15 ounces) Van Camp's® New Orleans Style Red Kidney Beans	1/2 cup chopped green pepper
2/3 cup shredded carrots	1/4 cup chopped onion
	1/2 cup mayonnaise
	1 teaspoon lemon juice

Drain kidney beans, reserving liquid. Combine beans, carrots, green pepper, and onion; set aside. Add reserved liquid to mayonnaise with lemon juice; fold into bean mixture. Chill several hours.   *5 servings*

SAUERKRAUT SALAD

A refreshing treat with a heavy meal.

1 can (16 ounces) Stokely's Finest® Shredded Sauerkraut, rinsed and drained	1 cup chopped onion
1 jar (4 ounces) Stokely's Finest® Sliced Pimientos, drained and chopped	1 green pepper, diced
	1/2 cup cider vinegar
	1/2 cup sugar

Combine all ingredients; mix well. Refrigerate overnight.
2 1/2 cups

ASPARAGUS VINAIGRETTE

A quick salad.

1 Tablespoon sugar
1 teaspoon salt
1 teaspoon paprika
1 teaspoon dry mustard
1/4 teaspoon pepper
1/4 cup cider vinegar
3/4 cup vegetable oil
Dash onion powder
1 Tablespoon sweet pickle
relish

1 Tablespoon chopped
Stokely's Finest®
Sliced Pimientos
1 can (14 1/2 ounces)
Stokely's Finest®
Cut Asparagus Spears,
drained
Hard-cooked eggs
(optional)

Combine sugar, salt, paprika, mustard, pepper, vinegar, oil, onion powder, pickle relish, and pimientos in a jar with a tight lid. Shake to mix well. Pour dressing over well drained asparagus and let marinate in refrigerator several hours before serving. Garnish with chopped hard-cooked eggs if desired.   *4 servings*

COOL CORN SALAD

Perfect to serve at picnics or at home.

1/4 cup commercial sour
cream
1/4 cup mayonnaise
1 Tablespoon prepared
mustard
2 teaspoons white vinegar
1 teaspoon sugar
1/4 teaspoon salt
1/8 teaspoon pepper
1 can (17 ounces)
Stokely's Finest®
Whole Kernel Golden
Corn, drained

1 jar (2 ounces)
Stokely's Finest®
Sliced Pimientos,
drained and diced
2 carrots, peeled and
grated
1/2 cup diced onion

In medium-size bowl, make dressing by combining sour cream, mayonnaise, mustard, vinegar, sugar, salt, and pepper. Add remaining ingredients and toss to blend. Cover and refrigerate at least 1 hour.   *4 to 6 servings*

TANGY BEAN SALAD

A delicious salad that can be assembled in 5 minutes to serve later. It keeps well in the refrigerator.

1/2 cup white vinegar	1 can (15 1/2 ounces)
1/2 cup sugar	Stokely's Finest®
1/2 cup vegetable oil	Cut Wax Beans,
1/2 cup chopped onion	drained
1/2 cup chopped green pepper	1 can (15 ounces)
1 can (16 ounces)	Stokely's Finest®
Stokely's Finest®	Dark Red Kidney
Cut Green Beans,	Beans, drained
drained	Red onion rings (optional)

Combine vinegar, sugar, oil, onion, and green pepper in large bowl and mix well. Drain all beans and add to dressing. Toss gently and marinate in refrigerator for at least 4 hours or overnight. Serve in bowl lined with lettuce. May be garnished with onion rings.
10 servings

FIESTA CHICKEN SALAD

A company treat that is so easy you'll make it for family meals.

1/2 cup mayonnaise or	1 can (30 ounces)
salad dressing	Stokely's Finest®
1 Tablespoon milk or	Fruit Cocktail,
cream	chilled and drained
1 teaspoon lemon juice	1/4 cup toasted, slivered
1/4 teaspoon nutmeg	almonds
1/8 teaspoon curry powder	
2 whole cooked chicken	
breasts, diced into	
1/2-inch cubes	

Blend together mayonnaise, milk, lemon juice, nutmeg, and curry powder. Fold in chicken and chill 30 minutes. When ready to serve, add fruit cocktail and almonds. Serve on bed of lettuce.
4 to 6 servings

Opposite: Cool Corn Salad (page 129), Tangy Bean Salad, Fiesta Chicken Salad

GREEN BEAN CRUNCHIES WITH TANGY DRESSING

Refreshing for buffet or luncheon.

1 can (16 ounces)
Stokely's Finest®
Sliced French Style
Green Beans
1 package (3 ounces)
lemon-flavored gelatin
1 envelope unflavored
gelatine

1/4 cup cold water
1/2 cup finely chopped
onion
1/2 cup chopped celery
1/2 cup coarsely chopped
walnuts or pecans

Tangy Dressing:

1/2 cup grated, drained,
unpeeled cucumber
1 cup mayonnaise
1/2 cup finely chopped
green pepper

2 teaspoons white vinegar
1/2 teaspoon salt
Dash pepper

Drain beans, reserving liquid. Add enough water to liquid to make 2 cups. Bring liquid to boil and add lemon gelatin, stirring until dissolved. Dissolve unflavored gelatine in 1/4 cup cold water and add to lemon gelatin mixture. Cool until slightly thickened. Fold in remaining ingredients. Pour into 6-cup mold or 8 individual molds and chill until firm. Stir dressing ingredients together; chill. Unmold salad on crisp greens and serve with Tangy Dressing.   *8 servings*

SALAD ROMANO

Cool and refreshing.

1 package (16 ounces)
Frozen Stokely's®
Vegetables Romano™
1/2 teaspoon rosemary
1/4 cup vegetable oil

1/4 cup white vinegar
1/3 cup commercial sour
cream
Pepper to taste
Parsley (optional)

Prepare vegetables according to cooking directions, adding rosemary to water. Drain and place in bowl. Blend oil with vinegar and pour over vegetables. Cover and marinate in refrigerator several hours. Drain; stir in sour cream and pepper. Top with fresh sprig of parsley if desired.   *4 servings*

DEL SOL VINAIGRETTE

A vegetable treat.

2/3 cup vegetable oil
1/3 cup red wine vinegar
1 teaspoon salt
1/2 teaspoon sugar
1/8 teaspoon cayenne
1/4 teaspoon dry mustard
1 hard-cooked egg, chopped
5 Tablespoons chopped sweet pickle
1 jar (2 ounces) Stokely's Finest® Sliced Pimientos, drained and chopped
3 Tablespoons chopped green pepper
3 Tablespoons chopped onion
3 Tablespoons chopped chives
2 Tablespoons chopped cucumber
2 Tablespoons chopped parsley
1 package (16 ounces) Frozen Stokely's® Vegetables del Sol®

Put oil, vinegar, salt, sugar, cayenne, and mustard in medium-size jar with screw top; shake vigorously. Add remaining ingredients, except frozen vegetables; shake to blend and chill. Cook frozen vegetables according to package directions, drain and chill. When dressing and vegetables are chilled, combine them, cover, and return to refrigerator until serving time.   *6 to 8 servings*

NUTTY BEET SALAD

A pretty and snappy salad.

1 jar (16 ounces) Stokely's Finest® Sliced Pickled Beets
1 package (3 ounces) mixed fruit-flavored gelatin
1 cup boiling water
2/3 cup cold water
1/4 cup chopped pecans
1/3 cup chopped celery

Drain beets, reserving 2 Tablespoons liquid. Dissolve gelatin in boiling water. Add cold water and reserved beet liquid. Cool until slightly thickened. Dice beets and fold beets, pecans, and celery into gelatin. Spoon into 1-quart mold or 8 individual molds. Chill until set.   *8 servings*

SURPRISE SALAD

A terrific meat accompaniment.

1 can (16 ounces)
   Stokely's Finest®
   Tomatoes
1 package (3 ounces)
   raspberry-flavored
   gelatin

1 teaspoon grated onion
1/2 cup mayonnaise
1 teaspoon horseradish

Purée tomatoes in blender. Place tomatoes in measuring cup; add water if necessary to make 2 cups. Heat to boiling. Remove from heat and stir in gelatin until dissolved. Add onion, pour into 2-cup mold, and chill until firm. Blend mayonnaise and horseradish and serve as garnish. *6 servings*

PEA SALAD

A make-ahead favorite.

1 can (17 ounces)
   Stokely's Finest®
   Peas, drained
2 hard-cooked eggs,
   chopped
1/2 green pepper, chopped
1/2 cup chopped onion

1/4 cup diced American
   cheese
3 Tablespoons mayonnaise
1/4 teaspoon pepper
3 slices cooked bacon,
   crumbled

Combine peas, eggs, green pepper, onion, and cheese in serving dish. Fold in mayonnaise, season with pepper, and top with bacon. Chill several hours before serving. *6 servings*

BROCCOLI SPEARS WITH MUSTARD SAUCE

Delicious cold.

1 package (10 ounces)
   Frozen Stokely's®
   Broccoli Spears
1/3 cup mayonnaise

2 teaspoons prepared
   mustard
1 teaspoon sugar

Cook broccoli according to package directions; drain and chill. Combine remaining ingredients and mix thoroughly. Serve sauce over chilled broccoli. *3 to 4 servings*

Nice to know: Sauce may also be served over cooked cauliflower. For a tasty hot dish, serve vegetables piping hot and top with sauce at room temperature.

RED BEAN SALAD

An ideal salad to serve with hamburgers.

1 can (15 ounces) Stokely's Finest® Dark Red Kidney Beans, well drained	2 Tablespoons mayonnaise
	1 teaspoon sugar
1/4 cup chopped onion	1/2 teaspoon prepared mustard
2 hard-cooked eggs, chopped	1/2 teaspoon seasoned salt
1/4 cup sweet pickle relish	1/4 teaspoon salt
	Dash pepper

Combine all ingredients and refrigerate at least 1 hour before serving. *4 servings*

MAKE AHEAD CAULIFLOWER SALAD

A sweet cheese dressing complements this salad. Lettuce stays crisp until salad is tossed.

1/2 head lettuce, shredded	5 slices cooked bacon, crumbled
1/4 cup chopped onion	3/4 cup mayonnaise
1 can (16 ounces) Stokely's Finest® Cut Green Beans, drained	1/3 cup grated Parmesan cheese
1/2 head cauliflower, cut into small flowerets	3 Tablespoons sugar

In large serving bowl, layer lettuce, onion, beans, cauliflower, and bacon. Blend remaining ingredients and spread over top of salad. Cover and refrigerate 8 hours. Toss all ingredients before serving. *8 servings*

Nice to know: Salad may be made one evening and served the next.

ROYAL PEAR SALAD

A party dish you can fix in the morning or the day before.

1 cup boiling water
1 package (6 ounces)
    raspberry-flavored
    gelatin
2 cups cold water
1 can (16 ounces) whole
    cranberry sauce

1 can (29 ounces)
    Stokely's Finest®
    Bartlett Pear Halves,
    drained
1/2 cup chopped walnuts
1/2 teaspoon lemon juice

Stir gelatin into boiling water until dissolved. Add cold water and cranberry sauce. Stir to blend. Chill until almost set. Cut all but 3 pear halves into chunks; slice reserved pear halves and set aside. Stir pear chunks, nuts, and lemon juice into gelatin mixture. Pour into 6-cup mold. Chill at least 6 hours, or until firm. Unmold on bed of lettuce, garnish with sliced pears, and serve.   *7 to 8 servings*

CAULIFLOWER CAPER

A great way to serve cauliflower on a hot summer night.

1 package (10 ounces)
    Frozen Stokely's®
    Cauliflower
6 Tablespoons vegetable
    oil
2 Tablespoons tarragon
    vinegar
1 teaspoon lemon juice
1 clove garlic, finely
    minced

1 teaspoon Italian
    seasoning
2 teaspoons capers,
    drained
1 Tablespoon
    Stokely's Finest®
    Sliced Pimientos
1 Tablespoon chopped
    parsley

Prepare cauliflower according to package directions; drain and set aside to cool. Meanwhile, combine oil, vinegar, lemon juice, garlic, and Italian seasoning in glass jar with screw top; shake vigorously. Place cauliflower in serving bowl and pour dressing over, turning cauliflower to coat well. Cover and refrigerate several hours. Garnish with capers, pimientos, and parsley.   *3 to 4 servings*

Opposite: Royal Pear Salad

GRAPEFRUIT VELVET FLUFF

A salad with a refreshing flavor.

1 package (3 ounces)
   lime-flavored gelatin
1/4 cup sugar
3/4 cup boiling water
1 can (16 ounces)
   Stokely's Finest®
   Grapefruit Sections

2 cups frozen whipped
   topping, thawed

Dissolve gelatin and sugar in boiling water. Set aside. Drain liquid from can of grapefruit sections into measuring cup and add enough water to make 1 cup liquid. Stir into gelatin mixture. Chill until slightly thickened. Fold whipped topping into slightly thickened mixture. Cut grapefruit sections in half and fold into slightly thickened gelatin mixture. Spoon into 6 or 8 individual molds and chill until firm. Serve on crisp lettuce leaves.   *6 to 8 servings*

FROZEN FRUIT SALAD

Light and delicious.

1 cup whipping cream
2 teaspoons confectioners
   sugar
1 Tablespoon mayonnaise
1 package (3 ounces)
   cream cheese, softened

1 package (16 ounces)
   Frozen Stokely's®
   Mixed Fruit
1 cup chopped nuts
   (optional)
Salad dressing

Whip cream, adding sugar halfway through whipping; set aside. Cream mayonnaise and cream cheese in medium-size bowl. Fold in whipped cream, fruit, and nuts; pour mixture into 7 1/2×12-inch pan. Cover tightly and freeze. Remove from freezer, uncover, and let stand at room temperature 15 minutes before serving. Serve on bed of lettuce, topped with salad dressing if desired.   *6 servings*

PINK APPLESAUCE SALAD

As delicious as it is pretty.

1 Tablespoon red cinnamon
  candies
1 cup boiling water
1 package (3 ounces)
  cherry-flavored
  gelatin

1 can (16 1/2 ounces)
  Stokely's Finest®
  Applesauce
1 cup finely chopped
  celery
1/2 cup chopped nuts

Melt candies in boiling water; pour over gelatin to dissolve. Add applesauce and chill until slightly thickened. Fold in celery and nuts; place in 4-cup gelatin mold. Chill until firm.　*6 servings*

REFRESHING CORN SALAD

Delicious with ham.

1 can (17 ounces)
  Stokely's Finest®
  Whole Kernel Golden
  Corn, drained
1/2 medium-size green
  pepper, diced

1 cup sliced celery
1 cup diced fresh tomato
1/4 teaspoon salt
1/3 cup French dressing
  Salad greens
  Red onion rings
  (optional)

Combine corn, green pepper, celery, tomato, and salt with dressing. Chill. Serve on salad greens and garnish with onion rings.　*4 to 5 servings*

KRAUT RELISH

Tangy good.

1 can (16 ounces)
  Stokely's Finest®
  Chopped Sauerkraut,
  well drained
1/2 cup sugar
1/2 cup finely chopped
  celery

1/2 cup finely chopped
  green pepper
1/2 cup finely chopped
  carrot
1/4 cup finely chopped
  onion

Combine all ingredients; cover and chill 12 hours before serving.　*8 servings*

QUICK CORN RELISH

Wonderful with hamburgers.

1 package (16 ounces)
  Frozen Stokely's®
  Chuckwagon Corn
1/2 cup sugar
1 Tablespoon cornstarch
1/2 cup white vinegar

1/3 cup water
1 teaspoon celery seed
1 teaspoon turmeric
1/2 teaspoon mustard seed
1/2 teaspoon dry mustard

Cook corn according to package directions; drain. In saucepan combine sugar and cornstarch; stir in vinegar and water. Add corn and remaining ingredients. Cook, stirring constantly, until thickened and bubbly, about 3 to 4 minutes. Cover and chill thoroughly.   *About 1 pint*

BEET-PINEAPPLE SALAD

Cool and crunchy.

1 can (16 ounces)
  Stokely's Finest®
  Diced Beets
1 can (8 1/4 ounces)
  crushed pineapple
2 packages (3 ounces each)
  or 1 package (6
  ounces) lemon-flavored
  gelatin

2 cups boiling water
  Dash salt
1/4 cup diced celery
1/4 cup chopped walnuts

Drain beets and pineapple, reserving liquids. Add enough cold water to liquid to equal 1 1/2 cups. Dissolve gelatin in boiling water; add reserved liquid and salt; mix well. Chill until partially set. Fold in beets, pineapple, celery, and walnuts. Pour into 8 or 10 individual molds or one 6-cup mold. Chill until firm.   *8 to 10 servings*

A Potpourri of Surprises

BROCCOLI-CHICKEN QUICHE

It tastes so good you will want seconds.

- 1 package (10 ounces) Frozen Stokely's® Chopped Broccoli
- 1 9-inch unbaked pie shell, well chilled
- 1 cup shredded Swiss cheese
- 1 chicken breast, cooked, skinned, boned, and diced
- 4 scallions (green onions), diced, including tops

- 3 eggs, beaten
- 1 cup half-and-half
- 1/2 cup milk
- 1/2 teaspoon seasoned salt
- 1/8 teaspoon salt
  - Dash pepper
- 1/4 cup grated Parmesan cheese

Preheat oven to 375°F. Cook broccoli according to package directions; drain well; cool. Remove pie shell from refrigerator; sprinkle Swiss cheese on bottom. Add broccoli, diced chicken, and scallions. Blend eggs, half-and-half, milk, and seasonings. Pour egg mixture over broccoli. Sprinkle with Parmesan cheese. Bake 40 to 45 minutes, or until knife inserted comes out clean. Let stand 5 minutes before serving.   *4 servings*

Nice to know: Turkey may be substituted for chicken. Use about 2 cups.

BAKED FRUIT SAUCE

A spicy way to dress up a simple dessert.

2 Tablespoons butter or margarine	1 cup water (3/4 cup in microwave method)
3/4 cup firmly packed brown sugar	1 package (16 ounces) Frozen Stokely's® Mixed Fruit
2 Tablespoons cornstarch	
1/2 teaspoon curry powder	

Preheat oven to 350°F. Melt butter in saucepan. Stir brown sugar, cornstarch, and curry into butter. Slowly add 1 cup water, stirring constantly until mixture comes to a boil. Boil 2 minutes. Place frozen fruit in 1 1/2-quart casserole and pour heated sauce over. Bake 1 hour. Serve hot or warm over pound cake, ice cream, or yogurt.   *About 1 1/2 cups*

Microwave Method: Melt butter in microwave oven in 4-cup measure. Stir brown sugar, cornstarch, and curry into butter. Slowly add 3/4 cup water, stirring constantly. Microcook 2 minutes, stirring after 1 minute. Place frozen fruit in 1 1/2-quart casserole and pour heated sauce over. Cover and microcook 10 to 12 minutes, stirring every 3 minutes. Serve hot or warm over pound cake, ice cream, or yogurt.

BEET CONSERVE

Delicious hot or cold with meat and poultry.

1 can (16 ounces) Stokely's Finest® Diced Beets, drained	1 teaspoon lemon juice
	1/4 teaspoon grated orange peel
1 can (16 1/2 ounces) Stokely's Finest® Applesauce	1 cup sugar
	1/4 cup raisins
	1/8 teaspoon ginger

Purée beets; add remaining ingredients. Cook over moderate heat, stirring several times, until mixture is thickened, about 45 minutes.   *2 2/3 cups*

Microwave Method: Purée beets; add remaining ingredients. Place in 1 1/2-quart casserole. Cover and microcook 12 minutes, or until thickened, stirring 3 times.

MEXICAN CORN BREAD

This very different corn bread has been a favorite of Mrs. W.B. Stokely III for years.

1 1/3 cups yellow cornmeal
1 1/3 cups all-purpose flour
3 Tablespoons sugar
1/2 teaspoon baking soda
1 teaspoon salt
2 eggs
1 cup buttermilk
1 can (8 1/2 ounces) Stokely's Finest® Cream Style Golden Corn
2 Tablespoons bacon drippings
1 medium-size onion, finely chopped
6 strips bacon, cooked and crumbled
3/4 cup grated American cheese, divided
1 to 2 Tablespoons chopped green chilies

Preheat oven to 400°F. Butter 9-inch square pan. Combine cornmeal, flour, sugar, baking soda, and salt in large mixing bowl. Beat eggs and stir in buttermilk, corn, bacon drippings, onion, bacon, 1/2 cup cheese, and chilies. Add to cornmeal mixture; stir until well combined. Pour batter into prepared pan and sprinkle with remaining 1/4 cup cheese. Bake 45 minutes. *8 to 10 servings*

BLUEBERRY MUFFINS

A wonderful breakfast treat.

3 cups all-purpose flour
1 1/4 cups sugar, divided
2 1/2 teaspoons baking powder
1 teaspoon salt
1 teaspoon cinnamon
1 teaspoon nutmeg
2 eggs, beaten
1 cup milk
2/3 cup vegetable oil
1 package (16 ounces) Frozen Stokely's® Whole Blueberries

Preheat oven to 400°F. Line 24 muffin cups with paper baking cups. Sift flour, 1 cup sugar, baking powder, salt, cinnamon, and nutmeg into mixing bowl. Make well in center of dry ingredients and add eggs, milk, and oil. Stir quickly and lightly until just mixed. Gently fold blueberries into batter. Fill baking cups two-thirds full. Bake 15 to 20 minutes. Remove from pan and sprinkle with remaining 1/4 cup sugar. *24 muffins*

TROPICAL OMELET

Try this colorful recipe for brunch or light suppers.

Fruit Sauce:

1 can (17 ounces)
  Stokely's Finest®
  Fruit Cocktail
1/3 cup orange juice

1 Tablespoon honey
2 teaspoons lemon juice
2 teaspoons cornstarch
1/2 banana, sliced

Omelet:

6 eggs
2 Tablespoons milk
1/2 teaspoon salt

Dash pepper
2 Tablespoons butter or
  margarine

Drain fruit cocktail reserving 2 Tablespoons liquid. In saucepan, blend reserved fruit cocktail liquid with orange juice, honey, lemon juice, and cornstarch. Cook over medium heat, stirring constantly, until thickened and bubbling. Stir in fruit cocktail and banana; heat until warmed through. Keep warm while preparing omelet.

1 large or 3 individual omelets

You may wish to make one large omelet or three individual omelets. To prepare: beat together eggs, milk, salt, and pepper. Melt butter in pan(s) for making omelet; when butter bubbles, add egg mixture to pan. Reduce heat to low and cook without stirring. As mixture begins to set, gently lift edges, allowing thin uncooked portion to flow to bottom. Cook until eggs are set. Remove to serving platter. Top with fruit filling and fold omelet in half. Serve at once.

Nice to know: Sprinkle Tropical Omelet with shredded Cheddar cheese for an added taste treat.

Opposite: Blueberry Muffins (page 143), Stokely's Finest® Orange Juice, Tropical Omelet

ORANGEY PUMPKIN BREAD

A bread with unusual taste and moist texture.

2/3 cup vegetable shortening	3 1/3 cups all-purpose flour
2 2/3 cups sugar	2 teaspoons baking soda
1 orange	1 1/2 teaspoons salt
2/3 cup water	1 teaspoon cinnamon
4 eggs	1 teaspoon cloves
1 can (16 ounces) Stokely's Finest® Pumpkin	1/2 teaspoon baking powder
	2/3 cup chopped pecans
	2/3 cup raisins or chopped dates

Grease two 9×5×3-inch loaf pans. Preheat oven to 350°F. Cream shortening and sugar thoroughly. Cut whole orange into wedges and remove seeds; place in blender with water and purée. Add orange mixture, eggs, and pumpkin to sugar mixture. Sift together flour, baking soda, salt, cinnamon, cloves, and baking powder. Add to pumpkin mixture. Stir in pecans and raisins or dates. Pour into prepared loaf pans and bake 1 hour and 10 minutes.   *2 loaves*

Nice to know: Pour batter into seven greased 16-ounce vegetable cans and bake at 350°F. 35 to 40 minutes, or until bread tests done. Ideal gifts.

PUFFY CORN FRITTERS

Delicious with warm maple syrup.

1 1/3 cups all-purpose flour	1 egg, well beaten
1 1/2 teaspoons baking powder	1 can (17 ounces) Stokely's Finest® Whole Kernel Golden Corn, well drained
3/4 teaspoon salt	
1 Tablespoon sugar	
2/3 cup milk	

Sift together flour, baking powder, salt, and sugar. Blend milk and egg; add gradually to dry ingredients. Stir in corn and drop from Tablespoon into deep hot fat (375°F.). Fry until golden brown, about 4 to 8 minutes, depending on size. Drain on paper towels and serve with warm maple syrup.   *16 to 20 fritters*

Opposite: Stokely's Finest® Orange Juice, Orangey Pumpkin Bread

CORN FLAPJACKS

Excellent served with honey or maple syrup.

2 cups sifted all-purpose
   flour
2 1/2 teaspoons baking powder
1 teaspoon salt
2 eggs
2 cups milk

1/3 cup vegetable oil
1 can (17 ounces)
   Stokely's Finest®
   Whole Kernel Golden
   Corn, drained

Sift flour, baking powder, and salt together; set aside. Beat eggs slightly; add milk, oil, and corn. Add corn mixture to dry ingredients all at once, stirring just enough to moisten. Fry on lightly greased griddle, turning once. *12 6-inch flapjacks*

Nice to know: Top flapjacks with hot creamed chicken or turkey for an unusual brunch treat.

CORN MUFFINS

Serve with a hearty soup.

1 1/2 cups all-purpose flour
1 Tablespoon sugar
4 teaspoons baking powder
1/2 teaspoon salt
1 egg, beaten
1 can (8 1/2 ounces)
   Stokely's Finest®
   Cream Style Golden
   Corn

1/4 cup milk
2 Tablespoons vegetable
   oil

Preheat oven to 400°F. Grease 12 muffin cups. Sift flour, sugar, baking powder, and salt together. Combine egg, corn, milk, and oil; pour over flour mixture. Stir until dry ingredients are just moistened. Fill muffin cups two-thirds full. Bake 18 to 20 minutes. *12 muffins*

Nice to know: Use this recipe to make corn sticks, or bake 30 minutes in an 8-inch square dish and cut into squares.

BORDELAISE SAUCE

A French favorite.

1 pound fresh mushrooms, sliced	1/4 cup dry red wine
1 Tablespoon instant minced onion	1 bay leaf
	4 peppercorns
2 Tablespoons butter or margarine	2 teaspoons instant beef flavored bouillon
2 Tablespoons all-purpose flour	1/2 teaspoon chopped parsley
1 can (8 ounces) Stokely's Finest® Sliced Carrots	1/4 teaspoon salt
	1/8 teaspoon pepper
	Dash thyme

Sauté mushrooms and onion in butter; stir flour into mushroom mixture and set aside. Purée carrots, including liquid. Add enough water to carrots to equal 2 cups liquid. Add puréed carrots to mushroom mixture; add remaining ingredients. Simmer 20 to 30 minutes, or until slightly thickened. Remove bay leaf and serve.
3 cups sauce

Nice to know: This sauce is delicious stirred in with thin strips of cooked round steak, flank steak, or leftover warmed beef, and served over cooked noodles.

BASIC SYRUP FOR POPCORN

3/4 cup sugar	2 quarts popped Popeye Popcorn (about 1/3 cup unpopped)
1/4 cup light corn syrup	
3 Tablespoons water	

In small saucepan combine sugar, corn syrup, and water. Stir continuously until mixture boils. Cook without stirring to 285°F. on a candy thermometer. Place popcorn in large greased mixing bowl. Pour syrup over popcorn and mix with greased wooden spoon until corn is well covered. Grease hands and immediately shape into desired form.   *Coating for 2 quarts popped popcorn*

Nice to know: If tinting is desired, add a few drops of food coloring to water when making syrup.

POPCORN SNOWMAN

4 quarts popped Popeye
  Popcorn (about 2/3 cup
  unpopped), divided
2 recipes Basic Syrup for
  Popcorn, cooked one
  at a time
  Toothpicks
1 12-inch wooden skewer
  (optional)

5 large gumdrops
6 small gumdrops
2 raisins
2 strings red licorice
1 foot of ribbon
2 lollipops (optional)

Place 2 quarts popped popcorn in large greased bowl. Prepare 1 recipe syrup and pour over popcorn, stirring with greased wooden spoon. Make 1 large ball 5 1/2 inches in diameter. Place on waxed paper to harden. Place remaining 2 quarts popcorn in bowl. Make second recipe of syrup and pour over popcorn. Shape into a 4-inch ball and a 3 1/2-inch ball. Place on waxed paper to harden.

To assemble body: Insert 2 toothpicks in top of large ball. Set middle-size ball on toothpicks. Insert 2 toothpicks in top of middle-size ball and set small ball in place. To provide stability, insert 12-inch skewer down through all 3 balls.

Hat: To make brim, place 2 large gumdrops together on sugar-sprinkled surface and flatten with rolling pin. Round edge with cookie cutter. To make crown, cut 2 large gumdrops in half, then press both flat pieces and 1 rounded end together. Cut sugar coating off bottom and press firmly onto brim. To trim hat, cut small gumdrop in half and fasten both pieces close together on brim with toothpicks. Place hat on snowman and secure with more toothpicks.

Features: Use half a toothpick to fasten features to snowman by inserting toothpick in feature, then pressing firmly into snowman. Cut 2 small gumdrops in half. Use rounded end for nose and 3 remaining pieces for buttons; use raisins for eyes. Cut 2-inch piece of red licorice for mouth. To make pipe (optional), twist a piece of red licorice around toothpick for pipestem. Use large gumdrop, rounded end down, for pipe bowl. Tie ribbon around neck for scarf. Insert lollipops for arms, if desired.   *1 snowman*

*Opposite: Decorated Popcorn Wreath (page 152), Popcorn Snowman, Orange Gatorade®
thirst quencher*

DECORATED POPCORN WREATH

2 quarts popped Popeye
  Popcorn (about 1/3 cup
  unpopped)
1 recipe Basic Syrup for
  Popcorn

1/4 teaspoon green food
  coloring
  About 35 small gumdrops
1 yard red ribbon

Grease a 6-cup ring mold and set aside. Place popped popcorn in large greased bowl. Prepare basic syrup, adding food coloring. Pour syrup over popcorn and stir with greased wooden spoon until popcorn is coated evenly. *Work very quickly* because syrup hardens fast. Grease hands and press popcorn mixture into prepared ring mold. Let stand at least 15 minutes to harden. Unmold and decorate with gumdrops held in place with toothpicks and ribbon tied in a bow. To display, loop another length of ribbon through center of wreath and use to hang.   *1 wreath*

CANDIED POPCORN ORNAMENTS

2 quarts popped Popeye
  Popcorn (about 1/3 cup
  unpopped)

1 recipe Basic Syrup for
  Popcorn, tinted if
  desired

Place popped popcorn in large greased bowl. Prepare syrup. Pour syrup over popcorn and stir with greased wooden spoon to coat popcorn evenly. Grease hands and immediately press mixture into six balls. Work very quickly because syrup hardens fast. Place balls on waxed paper and let stand at least 15 minutes to harden. Make hangers using thin ribbons of various colors wrapped around ornaments twice, tied with a loop at the top.   *6 3-inch balls*

POPCORN GARLAND

1 quart popped Popeye
  Popcorn (about 3
  Tablespoons unpopped)

7 feet of thread

To make garland use fine needle and long thread with knot in end. One quart of popped corn will make a 6-foot garland, or the garland may be lengthened by stringing a cranberry between each kernel of popcorn.   *6 feet*

LARGE CHRISTMAS TREE

4 quarts popped Popeye
    Popcorn (about 2/3 cup
    unpopped)
2 recipes Basic Syrup
    for Popcorn

1/2 pound gumdrops

Place popped popcorn in large greased bowl. Prepare syrup. Pour syrup over popcorn and stir with greased wooden spoon to coat popcorn evenly. Grease hands and immediately press syrup-coated corn together to build Christmas tree 12 inches tall. Make base about 6 inches in diameter. Then form popcorn tree to a point. Use gumdrops for ornaments and secure them with toothpicks. Make a gumdrop star for top of tree.   *1 tree*

Nice to know: Four hands help with this project; find a friend to help.

BUTTER CRISP TOPPING

Adds crunch to ice cream.

1 1/2 Tablespoons butter or
    margarine
1 1/2 Tablespoons brown sugar

1/2 cup Popeye Puffed Rice
1/4 cup slivered almonds

Melt butter in skillet; add brown sugar and heat until bubbly. Remove from heat and stir in Puffed Rice and almonds. Cool on waxed paper. Break into small pieces. Use as a crunchy ice cream topping.   *4 to 6 servings*

RANCH-STYLE EGGS

Spicy and unusual.

1 clove garlic, minced	1 can (16 ounces)
2 Tablespoons chopped	Stokely's Finest®
green chili pepper	Whole Tomatoes,
1 package (16 ounces)	drained
Frozen Stokely's®	1 1/2 teaspoons salt
Chuckwagon Corn	1 teaspoon oregano
2 Tablespoons butter or	6 eggs
margarine	English muffins
	(optional)

Preheat oven to 400°F. Sauté garlic, chili pepper, and corn in butter until corn is completely defrosted. Remove from heat and add tomatoes, salt, and oregano. Pour into greased 10×6×2-inch baking dish and place raw eggs, evenly spaced, on top. Bake until eggs are set, about 15 minutes. Serve over or alongside English muffins, if desired.   *6 servings*

GYPSY SCRAMBLE

A quick but substantial meal.

1/2 pound bacon	8 eggs, well beaten
1 green pepper, chopped	1 Tablespoon all-purpose
1 can (17 ounces)	flour
Stokely's Finest®	1/4 teaspoon salt
Cream Style Golden	1/8 teaspoon pepper
Corn	

Cook bacon until crisp. Drain, reserving 2 Tablespoons drippings in pan. Add green pepper to drippings and cook until tender, about 5 minutes. Combine remaining ingredients and add to skillet. Cook over moderate heat, stirring occasionally, until eggs are desired doneness. Stir in crumbled bacon and serve immediately.
4 to 5 servings

Another way: Serve over toast points and sprinkle crumbled bacon over eggs instead of stirring into egg mixture.

Desserts

GUM DROP CAKE

A mock fruit cake . . . great! Keeps well.

1 cup butter or margarine
2 cups sugar
2 eggs, beaten
4 cups sifted all-purpose
    flour
1 teaspoon cinnamon
1/4 teaspoon cloves
1/4 teaspoon nutmeg
1/4 teaspoon salt
1 teaspoon baking soda

1 can (16 ounces)
    Stokely's Finest®
    Applesauce
1 teaspoon vanilla extract
1 to 2 pounds small gum
    drops (minus licorice
    flavor)
1 box (15 ounces) golden
    raisins
1 1/2 cups chopped pecans

Grease and flour a 10-inch tube pan. Preheat oven to 325°F. Cream butter and sugar; add beaten eggs and mix well. Sift together flour, spices, salt, and baking soda; add to creamed mixture alternately with applesauce. Stir in remaining ingredients. Pour into prepared pan. Bake 1 hour; reduce heat to 300°F. and continue baking another 1 1/2 to 2 hours, or until cake tests done. Let cool in pan 20 to 25 minutes. Carefully invert cake on rack and cool completely.   *12 to 14 servings*

CHOCO-MOIST CAKE

An unusual and tasty flavor combination.

2 1/4 cups all-purpose flour
2 teaspoons baking soda
1 teaspoon salt
1 cup firmly packed
   brown sugar
2 eggs
1/4 cup butter or margarine,
   softened

1 can (17 ounces)
   Stokely's Finest®
   Fruit Cocktail,
   undrained
1 teaspoon cinnamon
1 package (6 ounces)
   semi-sweet chocolate
   pieces
3/4 cup chopped nuts

Preheat oven to 350°F. Grease and flour 13×9×2-inch pan. In large mixer bowl, combine all ingredients except chocolate pieces and nuts. Blend well at lowest speed; beat 2 minutes at medium speed. Pour batter into prepared pan. Sprinkle with chocolate and nuts. Bake 35 to 40 minutes. Cool in pan; cut into squares and serve.   *12 to 15 servings*

BLACK FOREST CHERRY CAKE

You'll take a prize with this one.

1 2-layer devil's food
   cake mix
   (not extra-moist
   or pudding-added
   cake mix)
3/4 cup water
1 1/2 cups granulated sugar,
   divided
1/2 cup plus 3 Tablespoons
   kirsch, divided
1 package (3 ounces)
   cream cheese,
   softened

2 cups confectioners
   sugar, divided
1 can (16 ounces)
   Stokely's Finest®
   Red Sour Pitted
   Cherries
5 Tablespoons cornstarch
   Red food coloring
2 cups whipping cream
   Chocolate curls

Make cake the day before it is to be served. Prepare cake according to package directions for two 8-inch layers. Boil water and 1/2 cup granulated sugar together in saucepan for 5 minutes, stirring frequently. Cool; stir in 1/4 cup kirsch. Leaving cake in pans, prick cake layers with fork and pour syrup evenly over both layers. Let stand overnight.

Beat cream cheese with 1 1/2 cups confectioners sugar until smooth. Set aside.

Drain cherries, reserving liquid. Place reserved liquid in saucepan with 1 cup granulated sugar, cornstarch, 1/4 cup kirsch, and a few drops red food coloring. Cook until very thick and clear. Stir in cherries; cool completely.

Whip cream until slightly thickened. Add 1/2 cup confectioners sugar and continue beating until stiff. Fold in 3 Tablespoons kirsch.

To assemble: Handle cake carefully as it is tender. Top one cake layer with half the cream cheese mixture, then half the cherry filling. Repeat with second layer. Cover top and sides of cake with whipped cream. Garnish with chocolate curls. Refrigerate until ready to serve.   *12 servings*

APPLESAUCE FRUIT CAKE

A traditional favorite.

1 can (16 1/2 ounces) Stokely's Finest® Applesauce	1/2 teaspoon salt
	1/4 teaspoon cloves
	1 1/4 cups golden raisins
1 1/3 cups sugar	1 cup chopped dates
2/3 cup butter or margarine	1 cup chopped pecans
2 3/4 cups all-purpose flour	1/2 cup halved candied cherries
2 1/2 teaspoons baking soda	
1 1/2 teaspoons cinnamon	1/2 cup candied fruits and citron
1/2 teaspoon nutmeg	

Grease and flour a 10-inch tube pan. Combine applesauce, sugar, and butter in saucepan and boil 5 minutes. Remove from heat and chill 45 to 60 minutes. Preheat oven to 275°F. Sift dry ingredients into large mixing bowl; add raisins, dates, pecans, cherries, and candied fruits, mixing thoroughly with dry ingredients. Blend in chilled applesauce mixture. Pour batter into prepared pan. Bake 2 hours or until a toothpick inserted in cake comes out clean. Cool 30 minutes in pan. Invert on rack and finish cooling.   *3 1/2 pound cake*

Nice to know: You'll find that a cake tester is a bit more reliable than a toothpick for deep cakes.

FRUIT COCKTAIL CAKE

A family favorite.

1 1/2 cups all-purpose flour
1 Tablespoon butter or margarine
1 cup granulated sugar
3/4 teaspoon salt
1 teaspoon baking soda
1 teaspoon vanilla extract
1/2 teaspoon almond extract
1 egg, lightly beaten

1 can (17 ounces) Stokely's Finest® Fruit Cocktail
1 cup chopped pecans, divided
3/4 cup firmly packed brown sugar
1 Tablespoon butter or margarine, softened
1 Tablespoon all-purpose flour

Preheat oven to 350°F. Grease and flour a 9-inch square pan. Blend flour, butter, granulated sugar, salt, baking soda, vanilla, almond extract, and egg with undrained fruit cocktail in electric mixer. Sprinkle 1/2 cup pecans in bottom of prepared pan. Top with batter. Combine brown sugar, softened butter, flour, and remaining 1/2 cup pecans to form coarse crumbs; sprinkle over batter. Bake 40 minutes. Cool in pan; cut into squares and serve.   *12 servings*

STRAWBERRY SOUR CREAM BUNDT CAKE

A rich cake for strawberry lovers.

1 package (16 ounces) Frozen Stokely's® Whole Strawberries without syrup, slightly thawed
1 package (18 1/2 ounces) yellow cake mix

1 cup commercial sour cream
4 eggs
1/2 cup currant jelly
2 teaspoons cornstarch
1 teaspoon almond extract

Preheat oven to 350°F. Grease and flour a 12-cup bundt cake pan. Slice strawberries, reserving half to make topping. Combine cake mix, sour cream, and eggs in large mixing bowl. Blend at low speed of electric mixer; beat at medium speed 2 minutes. Lightly fold half the sliced strawberries into batter (avoid vigorous stirring). Pour batter into prepared pan and bake 35 to 40 minutes, or until toothpick inserted into cake comes out clean. Cool cake in pan 15 minutes; invert onto cake rack until thoroughly cooled. Meanwhile, combine remaining strawberries and jelly in medium-size saucepan, cook over low heat, stirring constantly, until jelly is dissolved. Sprinkle cornstarch over strawberry mixture and cook until thickened. (Mixture should be of spreading consistency. If it is too thick, add 1 to 2 Tablespoons water and stir.) Remove from heat and stir in almond extract. When cake is thoroughly cooled, spoon strawberry mixture over and let stand until set.   *18 to 24 servings*

CARROT CAKE

Friends will ask for this recipe.

3/4 cup butter or margarine	2 cups all-purpose flour
1 cup firmly packed brown sugar	1/4 teaspoon baking soda
	1 Tablespoon baking powder
1/4 cup granulated sugar	1 teaspoon salt
1 can (16 ounces) Stokely's Finest® Diced Carrots, drained	1/2 teaspoon cinnamon
	2/3 cup chopped pecans
	1/3 cup soured milk (1/3 cup milk plus 1 teaspoon vinegar)
2 eggs, lightly beaten	

Cream Cheese Frosting:

6 Tablespoons butter or margarine	1 Tablespoon milk
1 package (3 ounces) cream cheese	3 cups sifted confectioners sugar
1 1/2 teaspoons vanilla extract	

Preheat oven to 350°F. Grease and flour two 8-inch cake pans. Cream butter and sugars in large bowl. Purée carrots in blender or food processor. Add carrots and eggs to butter mixture. Sift dry ingredients, add nuts, and stir to mix. Add dry ingredients and milk alternately to carrot mixture. Pour into prepared cake pans and bake 35 minutes, or until cake tests done. Cool in cake pans 10 minutes; remove to wire rack and cool completely. Cream butter and cheese. Add remaining ingredients and mix until spreading consistency. Place one cake layer upside down on serving plate. Spread with frosting. Cover with second layer and frost.   *10 to 12 servings*

CHOCOLATE KRAUT CAKE

You lose all kraut flavor — cake is very moist and tasty.
Delicious!

2/3 cup butter or margarine,
    softened
1 1/2 cups sugar
3 eggs
1 teaspoon vanilla
    extract
2 1/4 cups all-purpose flour
1/2 cup unsweetened cocoa

1 teaspoon baking powder
1 teaspoon baking soda
1/4 teaspoon salt
1 cup water
1 can (8 ounces)
    Stokely's Finest®
    Shredded Sauerkraut,
    rinsed twice and
    drained well

Chocolate Cream Cheese Frosting:

1 package (3 ounces)
    cream cheese,
    softened
6 Tablespoons butter or
    margarine, at room
    temperature
1 1/2 teaspoons vanilla
    extract

6 Tablespoons unsweetened
    cocoa
3 cups sifted confectioners
    sugar
3 Tablespoons milk

Preheat oven to 350°F. Grease and flour two 8-inch round cake pans. Cream butter and sugar; beat in eggs and vanilla. Sift together dry ingredients; add alternately with water to creamed mixture. Using kitchen shears, snip sauerkraut fine. Fold into cake batter. Pour into cake pans and bake 40 to 45 minutes, or until cake tests done. Cool in cake pans 10 minutes before removing. Remove from pans and cool completely before frosting.   *12 servings*

Frosting: Blend cream cheese and butter; add vanilla. Sift cocoa and confectioners sugar. Add sugar alternately with milk and beat until of spreading consistency. Frost cake.

PEAR UPSIDE DOWN CAKE

A different fruit goes upside down.

2 Tablespoons butter or margarine
1/2 cup firmly packed brown sugar
2 Tablespoons light corn syrup
1 can (16 ounces) Stokely's Finest® Sliced Bartlett Pears, drained
1/2 cup chopped pecans
1/4 cup quartered maraschino cherries

1 1/4 cups granulated sugar
1/2 cup butter or margarine, softened
1 1/2 teaspoons vanilla extract
2 eggs
1 1/3 cups all-purpose flour
1/3 cup cocoa
1/2 teaspoon baking soda
1/2 teaspoon salt
1/2 cup buttermilk

Preheat oven to 350°F. In oven, melt butter in 9-inch square pan. Add brown sugar and corn syrup; mix well and spread evenly over bottom of pan. Arrange pears in pan and sprinkle with pecans and cherries; set aside. Cream granulated sugar, softened butter, and vanilla. Add eggs, beating in one at a time. Combine flour, cocoa, baking soda, and salt; add alternately with buttermilk to butter mixture. Pour over pears and bake 45 to 50 minutes. Invert cake onto serving plate immediately.   *9 to 12 servings*

QUICK AND EASY STRAWBERRY SHORTCAKE

The brandy adds an extra kick.

1 package (16 ounces) Frozen Stokely's® Strawberry Halves, in syrup, partially thawed
2 Tablespoons brandy

1 cup whipping cream
2 Tablespoons sugar
1/2 teaspoon vanilla extract
1 package sponge cake shells

Combine strawberries and brandy in medium-size bowl; stir gently. Whip cream until slightly thickened. Add sugar and vanilla and continue to whip until soft peaks form. Spoon strawberries into shells and top with heaping dollop of sweetened whipped cream.   *6 servings*

PEACH BAVARIAN CREAM

Absolutely delicious!

1 package (16 ounces)
   Frozen Stokely's®
   Sliced Peaches, thawed
1 cup boiling water
1 envelope unflavored
   gelatine

1 package (3 ounces)
   peach-flavored
   gelatin
1 cup whipping cream,
   whipped

Drain peaches, reserving liquid. Reserve a few slices for garnish and cut remaining peaches into pieces. Pour boiling water over gelatins, stirring until gelatin dissolves. Add enough water to reserved peach liquid to equal 1 cup; add to gelatin, stir to blend. Chill until almost set. Meanwhile, fold a 30-inch piece of foil lengthwise into a 3-inch-wide strip. Tape paper collar around outside of a 1-quart soufflé dish. Beat gelatin with mixer until foamy. Add peach pieces. Reserve 2 Tablespoons whipped cream for garnish; fold remainder into gelatin-peach mixture. Pour into soufflé dish. Chill until firm. Garnish with reserved peach slices and reserved whipped cream.   *4 servings*

PEACH HAY STACKS

Shredded wheat makes a toasty topping.

1/4 cup crushed shredded
     wheat
  2 Tablespoons butter or
     margarine, melted
  2 Tablespoons brown sugar
  2 Tablespoons shredded
     coconut

2 Tablespoons chopped
   pecans
1/4 teaspoon cinnamon
1 can (16 ounces)
   Stokely's Finest®
   Cling Peach Halves,
   well drained

Combine shredded wheat, butter, brown sugar, coconut, pecans, and cinnamon; mix well. Place peach halves, cut side up, in 11×8×2-inch pan. Spoon shredded wheat mixture into center of each peach half. Broil 3 minutes, or until lightly toasted. Serve at once.
6 servings

Opposite: Peach Bavarian Cream, Peach Hay Stacks

FLAMING CHERRIES JUBILEE WITH ICE CREAM

A dramatic company dessert.

1 package (16 ounces)
  Frozen Stokely's®
  Dark Sweet Cherries,
  thawed
1/4 cup rum
1 Tablespoon cornstarch

1/2 cup currant jelly
1/2 teaspoon grated lemon
  peel (optional)
1/3 cup brandy
French vanilla ice
  cream

Drain cherries, reserving liquid. Place cherries in medium-size bowl. Add lemon peel, if desired. Pour rum over, cover, and refrigerate 3 hours. Place reserved cherry liquid in measuring cup and add enough water to make 3/4 cup. Place cornstarch in saucepan; slowly add cherry liquid, stirring constantly. Add jelly, and cook over medium heat, stirring until jelly dissolves and mixture is thickened. Add cherries with rum and lemon peel; cook, stirring constantly, about 3 minutes. Remove from heat and place in heat-proof serving dish. Warm brandy, ignite carefully, pour over cherry mixture, and spoon over ice cream. Serve immediately.
6 to 8 servings

PEACH CLOUDS

Pudding topped with sweet clouds.

1 package (3 3/4 ounces)
  vanilla flavor instant
  pudding and pie filling
1 can (16 ounces)
  Stokely's Finest®
  Cling Peach Halves,
  well-drained

2 Tablespoons chopped
  pecans
1 egg white
1/4 cup sugar
1/2 teaspoon white vinegar

Preheat oven to 350°F. Prepare pudding according to package directions. Pour pudding into 6 individual serving dishes and chill. Arrange 6 peach halves, cut side up, in greased 9-inch square baking dish. Place 1 teaspoon pecans in center of each peach half. Beat egg white until stiff but not dry; add sugar gradually and continue beating until smooth. Add vinegar and beat 1 minute. Spread meringue on top of each peach half and bake 15 to 20 minutes, or until lightly browned. To serve, place warm peach half on top of pudding.
6 servings

PEACH KUCHEN

Always a favorite.

1/2 cup butter or margarine
3/4 cup sugar
1 1/4 cups all-purpose flour
1/2 teaspoon salt
1/2 teaspoon cinnamon
1/4 teaspoon baking powder

1 can (29 ounces)
   Stokely's Finest®
   Sliced Cling Peaches,
   well drained
1 egg, beaten
1 cup whipping cream

Preheat oven to 375°F. Cream butter and sugar. Sift together dry ingredients. Add sifted mixture to creamed butter. Blend until crumbly; reserve 1/3 cup. Press remaining amount evenly in bottom and 1 inch up sides of ungreased 8-inch square pan. Arrange well-drained peach slices over crumbs. Sprinkle with reserved 1/3 cup crumbs and bake 15 minutes. Blend egg and cream and pour over peaches. Continue baking an additional 25 to 30 minutes, or until custard is set. Cool completely in pan.   *6 to 9 servings*

Another Way: Substitute 1 can (30 ounces) Stokely's Finest® Deluxe Whole Purple Plums, halved and pitted, for the peaches.

SPRING FLUFF

Refreshing as the season!

1 envelope unflavored
   gelatine
3/4 cup sugar
1 1/4 cups boiling water
1 teaspoon grated lemon
   or orange peel
1/4 cup lemon or orange
   juice

2 egg whites
1 package (10 ounces)
   Frozen Stokely's®
   Red Raspberries in
   syrup, thawed

Blend gelatine and sugar together; add boiling water and stir until completely dissolved. Add peel and juice; mix well. Chill mixture, stirring occasionally, until slight lumps form. Pour into large mixing bowl; add egg whites and beat on high speed of mixer until mixture is light and fluffy (5 to 10 minutes). Place fluffy mixture in large serving dish or in individual serving dishes and refrigerate until firm. Top with generous amount of raspberries in syrup for a light and colorful dessert.   *6 to 8 servings*

WARM FRUITFUL COMPOTE

Serve with cookies at your next buffet.

1/2 cup whole cranberry sauce	2 Tablespoons sugar
1 can (16 ounces) Stokely's Finest® Sliced Cling Peaches, drained	1/4 teaspoon cinnamon
	1/8 teaspoon cloves
	1/8 teaspoon nutmeg
1 can (16 ounces) Stokely's Finest® Sliced Bartlett Pears, drained	Whipped cream or frozen whipped topping (optional)
1 can (16 ounces) Stokely's Finest® Apricot Halves, drained	Walnut halves (optional)

In large skillet, heat cranberry sauce. Add peaches, pears, and apricots. Sprinkle with sugar, cinnamon, cloves, and nutmeg. Cover and heat 5 to 10 minutes, or until fruit is warmed through. Stir gently to blend flavors. Serve warm garnished with nuts and whipped cream or whipped topping.   *6 to 8 servings*

Microwave Method: Microcook cranberry sauce in 1 1/2-quart casserole for 1 1/2 minutes, uncovered. Add peaches, pears, and apricots. Sprinkle with sugar, cinnamon, cloves, and nutmeg. Microcook 2 minutes, uncovered. Stir mixture thoroughly but gently. Cover and microcook 1 additional minute. Serve warm, garnished with nuts and whipped cream or whipped topping.

Opposite: Warm Fruitful Compote

PEACHES SOUTHERN STYLE

A new way to serve peach pie.

2 cans (29 ounces each)
Stokely's Finest®
Sliced Cling Peaches,
drained
1 cup golden raisins
1/3 cup sweet bourbon
liqueur
2/3 cup sugar
1 cup plus 2 Tablespoons
all-purpose flour,
divided

3 Tablespoons butter or
margarine
1/2 teaspoon salt
1/3 cup vegetable shortening
1 Tablespoon water
1 egg
1/4 teaspoon white
vinegar

Preheat oven to 425°F. Place peaches and raisins in an 8-inch square baking dish. Pour liqueur over fruit. Combine sugar and 2 Tablespoons flour in bowl. Cut in butter until mixture resembles fine crumbs. Sprinkle over fruit. Combine remaining flour and salt; cut in shortening. Add water, egg, and vinegar; form mixture into ball. Refrigerate 10 minutes. Flour board and roll out pastry to 1/8 inch thickness; place over peaches. Slit top to allow steam to escape. Bake 10 minutes, then reduce heat to 350°F. and bake an additional 15 to 20 minutes. Serve warm.   *5 to 6 servings*

EASY CHERRY PUDDING

A joy to make.

1/2 cup butter or margarine
1 1/2 cups sugar, divided
1 cup all-purpose flour
2 teaspoons baking powder
3/4 cup milk

1 can (16 ounces)
Stokely's Finest®
Red Sour Pitted
Cherries

Preheat oven to 325°F. Melt butter in 9-inch square pan. Combine 1 cup sugar, flour, baking powder, and milk. Mix until well blended. Pour over melted butter; do not stir. Pour undrained cherries over batter; do not stir. Sprinkle remaining 1/2 cup sugar over cherries; do not stir. Bake 1 hour.   *8 servings*

Good idea: For a special treat, serve warm, topped with ice cream.

APPLESAUCE BARS

Moist bar cookies great for all ages. These keep well in the refrigerator.

2 1/2 cups all-purpose flour
1 cup sugar
1/4 teaspoon baking powder
1 1/2 teaspoons baking soda
1 1/2 teaspoons salt
3/4 teaspoon cinnamon
1/2 teaspoon cloves
1/2 teaspoon allspice
1/2 cup vegetable shortening, at room temperature

1/2 cup water
1 can (16 1/2 ounces) Stokely's Finest® Applesauce
1 egg
1/2 cup chopped nuts
1 cup chopped raisins

Caramel Frosting:

1/4 cup butter or margarine
1/2 cup firmly packed brown sugar

3 Tablespoons milk
About 1 1/2 cups sifted confectioners sugar

Preheat oven to 350°F. Grease and flour 15×10×1-inch jelly-roll pan. Sift all dry ingredients into a large mixing bowl. Add shortening, water, applesauce, and egg. Beat 4 minutes with electric mixer on medium speed. Gently fold in nuts and raisins. Pour into prepared pan and bake 30 minutes. Cool in pan. To make frosting, melt butter, add brown sugar; boil for 1 minute, stirring constantly. Cool slightly. Stir in milk. Gradually add confectioners sugar and beat until of spreading consistency. Frost cake in pan and cut into bars.
48 bars

COFFEE PEACH PARFAITS

A favorite of coffee lovers.

1 can (8 3/4 ounces) Stokely's Finest® Sliced Cling Peaches
1/2 teaspoon instant coffee

Dash nutmeg
Coffee, vanilla, or peach ice cream

Drain peach syrup into saucepan; add coffee and nutmeg; heat to boiling; cool. Layer ice cream, peach slices, and desired amount of syrup in dessert dishes. Serve with espresso.   *2 servings*

Nice to know: This recipe is so easy to make you can increase the amount, prepare it ahead of time, and serve it to company.

ALMOND-CHOCOLATE COATED PEARS

An elegant dessert, just right for company.

1 can (29 ounces)
Stokely's Finest®
Bartlett Pear Halves,
drained
2 Tablespoons butter
or margarine
3 squares (1 ounce each)
unsweetened baking
chocolate

3/4 cup sugar
1/2 cup whipping cream
1 egg yolk, beaten
3/4 teaspoon almond extract
1/3 cup slivered almonds

Drain pear halves on paper towel and refrigerate until ready to use. Melt butter and chocolate in heavy saucepan over low heat. Add sugar and cream, stirring constantly, until sugar dissolves, about 6 minutes. Remove from heat and stir 1 Tablespoon of chocolate mixture into beaten egg yolk; stir egg yolk mixture into remaining chocolate mixture. Add almond extract and stir. Let stand 10 minutes. Place 1 pear half in each individual serving dish. To serve, spoon chocolate mixture over pears and sprinkle with almonds. *6 to 8 servings*

Nice to know: Leftover sauce may be refrigerated for later use. Warm to serve.

TOP HAT PEARS

Pop this dessert in the oven to cook while you are eating the main course.

2 Tablespoons butter or
margarine, softened
2 Tablespoons brown sugar
1/4 cup oats, uncooked
1/4 cup chopped almonds
2 teaspoons grated lemon
peel

1 can (8 1/2 ounces)
Stokely's Finest®
Bartlett Pear Halves,
drained

Preheat oven to 400°F. Combine butter, sugar, oats, almonds, and lemon peel; blend well and set aside. Arrange pears in small baking dish, cut side up. Top each pear with rounded scoop of oats mixture. Bake 10 minutes. *2 to 3 servings*

STRAWBERRY-PEACH TRIFLE

An easy version of an old English dessert.

1 pound cake, cut into
　　1/2-inch slices
1/3 cup sweet sherry
1 package (3 3/4 ounces)
　　vanilla-flavored
　　instant pudding mix
1 package (16 ounces)
　　Frozen Stokely's®
　　Whole Strawberries
　　without syrup,
　　slightly thawed

1 package (16 ounces)
　　Frozen Stokely's®
　　Sliced Peaches,
　　slightly thawed
1 carton (4 1/2 ounces)
　　frozen whipped
　　topping, thawed
Mint leaves (optional)

Place pieces of pound cake in shallow pan, sprinkle with sherry, cover, and refrigerate. Meanwhile, prepare pudding according to package directions. Cut strawberries in half and peaches into chunks. Layer half the cake slices in an attractive glass serving bowl. Top with half the pudding, all the strawberries, and half the whipped topping. Repeat layers, using peaches in place of berries. Garnish top with mint leaves. Refrigerate for 1 hour before serving.
6 to 8 servings

BLUEBERRY CRISP

An after-school treat children will love.

1 package (16 ounces)
　　Frozen Stokely's®
　　Blueberries
1 Tablespoon lemon juice
3/4 cup all-purpose flour
1/2 cup granola
1/2 cup firmly packed brown
　　sugar

1/2 teaspoon cinnamon
　　(optional)
1/2 teaspoon nutmeg
　　(optional)
1/4 teaspoon salt
5 Tablespoons butter or
　　margarine, softened
Heavy cream

Preheat oven to 375°F. Place blueberries in bottom of 8-inch square baking dish and sprinkle with lemon juice. Combine flour, granola, sugar, cinnamon, nutmeg, and salt in medium-size bowl. Cut butter into flour mixture until mixture resembles coarse crumbs. Sprinkle over blueberries and bake 30 to 40 minutes, or until top is lightly browned. Serve warm with cream.　　*6 servings*

PEACH PIZZA

A winner everytime.

1 package (18 ounces)
  refrigerated sugar
  cookie dough
1 package (8 ounces)
  cream cheese, softened
4 Tablespoons sugar
1/2 teaspoon vanilla
  extract

1 package (16 ounces)
  Frozen Stokely's®
  Peaches, thawed
  and drained
2 bananas, sliced
1/4 cup apricot preserves
2 Tablespoons water
  (about)

Preheat oven to 375°F. Grease a 14-inch pizza pan. Slice cookie dough in 1/8-inch thick slices and completely line pizza pan with raw dough, overlapping slices. Bake 12 minutes. Cool completely. Blend cream cheese, sugar, and vanilla until smooth. Spread over cooled crust; top with well-drained peach slices and bananas, arranged decoratively. Blend apricot preserves and water; glaze fruit with mixture. Refrigerate until ready to use. Cut like a pizza.
8 servings

Nice to know: grapes, strawberries, bing cherries, or melon wedges may be used with the peaches.

STRAWBERRY CRÊPES

For variety, try a blueberry filling.

Crêpes:
1 cup all-purpose flour
2 Tablespoons sugar
1/4 teaspoon salt
1 1/4 cups milk
4 eggs, lightly beaten

1 Tablespoon vanilla
  extract or brandy
1 Tablespoon butter,
  melted

Filling:
3 egg whites
1 cup confectioners sugar
1/2 teaspoon grated orange
  peel
1/4 teaspoon vanilla
  extract

1/8 teaspoon almond extract
1 package (16 ounces)
  Frozen Stokely's®
  Whole Strawberries
  (without syrup)

Combine flour, sugar, and salt; stir in remaining ingredients except butter, beating until smooth. Cover and let stand in refrigerator at least 1 hour. Heat small skillet or 6-inch crêpe pan until hot. Brush pan lightly with butter. Pour in about 2 Tablespoons batter, rotating pan quickly to spread batter completely over bottom of pan. Cook over medium heat until lightly browned on bottom, about 1 minute. Turn and brown lightly on other side. Remove to waxed paper to cool.

To make filling: Beat egg whites; gradually add sugar and beat until stiff peaks form. Blend in orange peel and extracts. Fold in strawberries. Place about 1 Tablespoon filling on each crêpe, slightly off center; roll filled crêpe. Preheat oven to 450°F. Place crêpes in shallow oven-proof dish, seam side down. Bake 5 minutes; sprinkle each serving with confectioners sugar.   *About 20 crepes*

Nice to know: Batter can be made in blender or food processor and it will keep nicely in the refrigerator. If you are pressed for time, prepare batter one day and make crêpes the next day. Cooked crêpes can be stored in the freezer. Place a piece of waxed paper between each crêpe and overwrap with plastic wrap. Defrost before filling.

RHUBARB CRISP

Serve this delicious fruit crisp with vanilla ice cream.

1 cup granulated sugar	3/4 cup all-purpose flour
1 Tablespoon cornstarch	1/2 cup firmly packed
1/4 cup orange juice	brown sugar
1 package (20 ounces)	1/2 teaspoon cinnamon
Frozen Stokely's®	1/4 teaspoon ginger
Cut Rhubarb	1/4 cup butter or margarine

Preheat oven to 350°F. In large bowl combine sugar, cornstarch, and orange juice. Add rhubarb and mix well. Pour mixture into 8-inch square baking dish. Combine flour, brown sugar, cinnamon, and ginger. Cut butter into flour mixture until mixture resembles fine crumbs. Sprinkle on top of rhubarb. Bake 30 to 45 minutes.
6 servings

FRUITFUL TARTS WITH ORANGE GLACÉ

Oh what an easy, elegant dessert.

1/2 cup sugar
1 1/2 Tablespoons cornstarch
Dash salt
1/2 cup orange juice
4 Tablespoons water
1 package (16 ounces)
Frozen Stokely's®
Mixed Fruit,
slightly thawed

1 package (4 ounces)
6 ready-to-use
graham cracker tart
shells
Whipped cream (optional)

Place sugar, cornstarch, and salt in medium-size saucepan. Add orange juice and water; cook over medium heat, stirring constantly, until mixture thickens and boils. Let boil 1 minute, stirring; remove from heat and cool. Add fruit to cooled sauce and mix gently. Fill shells with fruit mixture and refrigerate until serving time. To serve, garnish each tart with dollop of whipped cream.   *6 servings*

SHERRIED FRUIT COMPOTE

Double this recipe next time you have a big party.

1 can (29 ounces)
Stokely's Finest®
Cling Peach Halves
1 can (29 ounces)
Stokely's Finest®
Bartlett Pear Halves
1 can (20 ounces)
pineapple chunks

3/4 cup firmly packed brown
sugar
1/2 cup dry sherry
Dash ginger
1/2 teaspoon cinnamon
6 Tablespoons butter or
margarine
1/4 cup lemon juice

Preheat oven to 350°F. Drain fruits; place in shallow baking dish. Combine remaining ingredients in saucepan and heat to boiling. Pour sauce over fruit. Bake, uncovered, 35 to 40 minutes, basting occasionally. Serve warm.   *10 servings*

MACAROON PEACHES

An easy hurry-up dessert.

1 can (16 ounces)
    Stokely's Finest®
    Cling Peach Halves
6 coconut macaroons
3 Tablespoons butter or
    margarine, melted

1 Tablespoon sugar
2 Tablespoons white wine
2 teaspoons grated
    orange peel

Thoroughly drain peach halves. Place in shallow baking dish, cut side up. Crumble macaroons into small bowl. Add butter, sugar, wine, and orange peel, stirring to blend. Sprinkle mixture over peach halves. Place under broiler and broil 10 minutes or until heated through. Serve warm.　　*6 servings*

PUMPKIN RUMKINS

The rum flavor adds a holiday touch.

1 can (16 ounces)
    Stokely's Finest®
    Pumpkin
1 cup firmly packed brown
    sugar
1/2 teaspoon salt
1 teaspoon cinnamon
1/2 teaspoon nutmeg

1/4 teaspoon ginger
4 eggs, lightly beaten
1 cup evaporated milk
1 teaspoon grated orange
    peel
3/4 cup orange juice
1 teaspoon rum extract

Sweetened Sour Cream:

2 Tablespoons sugar
1/4 teaspoon vanilla
    extract

1 cup commercial sour
    cream

Preheat oven to 350°F. Grease ten 6-ounce custard cups. Combine pumpkin, sugar, salt, cinnamon, nutmeg, ginger, and eggs; mix well. Stir in evaporated milk, orange peel, orange juice, and rum extract. Pour into prepared custard cups, filling each cup to about 1/2 inch from top. Set in shallow baking pan. Fill pan with hot water to depth of half the custard cups. Bake about 50 minutes, or until set. Cool. Serve with Sweetened Sour Cream. To make Sweetened Sour Cream: combine sugar, vanilla, and sour cream. Mix well and serve with Pumpkin Rumkins. Garnish with shredded orange peel if desired.　　*10 servings*

PEAR CRUNCH PIE

Terrific . . . and different!

1/4 cup sugar
2 Tablespoons cornstarch
1/8 teaspoon salt
1/8 teaspoon nutmeg
1 can (29 ounces)
   Stokely's Finest®
   Bartlett Pear Halves

1 Tablespoon lemon juice
1 Tablespoon butter
1 9-inch pie shell,
   unbaked

Topping:

1 cup quick-cooking oats,
   uncooked
1/3 cup firmly packed brown
   sugar
1/3 cup butter or margarine,
   melted

1/3 cup chopped pecans
1/4 teaspoon nutmeg
1/4 teaspoon cinnamon

Preheat oven to 425°F. In saucepan, combine sugar, cornstarch, salt, and nutmeg. Drain pears, reserving liquid. Add water to reserved liquid to make 1 1/2 cups; stir liquid into saucepan. Cook over medium heat, stirring constantly until mixture is thick and clear. Remove from heat and stir in lemon juice and butter. Slice pears and arrange in unbaked pie shell. Pour sauce over pears. Combine topping ingredients and sprinkle over pie. Bake 20 minutes.
8 servings

SCOTCHY PEACH SUNDAES

A quick party dessert: simple but wonderful.

1/3 cup butter or margarine
1 can (16 ounces)
   Stokely's Finest®
   Sliced Cling Peaches,
   drained

1/2 cup firmly packed brown
   sugar
   Vanilla ice cream
1/3 cup chopped pecans

Melt butter in skillet. Stir in peaches. Sprinkle brown sugar over peaches and stir gently. Simmer 5 minutes, or until bubbly. Serve warm over vanilla ice cream. Top with pecans.   *6 servings*

Opposite: Pear Crunch Pie, Pumpkin Rumkins (page 175)

CHIFFON STRAWBERRY PIE

Use frozen strawberries and serve this favorite all year 'round.

1 package (16 ounces)
   Frozen Stokely's®
   Whole Strawberries,
   in syrup, thawed
1 package (3 ounces)
   strawberry-flavored
   gelatin
1/4 cup water

1 cup whipping cream,
   divided
2 egg whites
1/4 teaspoon cream of
   tartar
1 ready-to-use 9-inch
   graham cracker pie
   crust

Drain strawberries; set berries aside; place liquid in measuring cup, add enough water to make 1 cup. Bring liquid to a boil, remove from heat, add gelatin and stir to dissolve. Stir in 1/4 cup cold water. Mash reserved strawberries and stir in. Cool until egg-white consistency. Whip 1/2 cup cream and fold into chilled strawberry mixture. Meanwhile, beat egg whites and cream of tartar until stiff peaks form. Gently fold into strawberry mixture. Pour mixture into prepared pie shell and refrigerate several hours. To serve, whip remaining 1/2 cup cream and spoon on top of pie.   *6 servings*

GOLDEN NUGGET PIE

Different and very good.

1 can (30 ounces)
   Stokely's Finest®
   Fruit Cocktail
1/2 cup firmly packed
   brown sugar
2 Tablespoons cornstarch

1 teaspoon lemon juice
2 Tablespoons butter or
   margarine
1/8 teaspoon salt
   Pastry for 9-inch pie
   shell and lattice top

Preheat oven to 425°F. Drain fruit cocktail, reserving 3/4 cup liquid. Blend sugar and cornstarch; add to reserved liquid. Cook and stir until thickened. Add fruit cocktail, lemon juice, butter, and salt. Pour into unbaked pie shell. Put lattice top in place. Bake 10 minutes; reduce heat to 350°F. and bake an additional 35 minutes.
6 to 8 servings

PUMPKIN PECAN PIE

A Fall favorite!

1 can (18 ounces)
   Stokely's Finest®
   Pumpkin Pie Filling
1 cup evaporated milk
2 eggs
1 unbaked 9-inch
   pie shell

2 Tablespoons butter or
   margarine, melted
1/4 cup firmly packed brown
   sugar
3/4 cup chopped pecans

Preheat oven to 450°F. Blend together pumpkin, milk, and eggs; pour into pie shell. Bake 10 minutes; reduce heat to 350°F. and bake an additional 30 minutes. Meanwhile, combine butter and sugar; stir in pecans. Spoon pecan mixture into pie shell. Bake an additional 20 minutes, or until a knife inserted in center comes out clean.
8 servings

SOUR CREAM PUMPKIN PIE

So good!

3/4 cup firmly packed
   brown sugar
1/2 teaspoon salt
1 Tablespoon all-purpose
   flour
1/2 teaspoon cinnamon
1/4 teaspoon ginger
1/8 teaspoon cloves
1/4 teaspoon nutmeg

2 eggs, lightly beaten
1 can (16 ounces)
   Stokely's Finest®
   Pumpkin
1 cup evaporated milk
1/2 cup water
1 9-inch pie shell,
   unbaked

Topping:

3 1/2 Tablespoons sugar
1 teaspoon vanilla extract

1 cup commercial sour
   cream

Preheat oven to 450°F. Thoroughly mix brown sugar, salt, flour, and spices. Add eggs and pumpkin; mix until well blended. Stir in milk and water and pour into pie shell. Bake 20 minutes. Reduce heat to 350°F. and continue baking 20 minutes longer until firm, or when knife inserted in middle comes out clean. Remove from oven, leaving oven turned on. Cool pie 5 minutes while you make topping. Combine sugar, vanilla, and sour cream. Spread on pie. Return pie to oven for an additional 10 minutes. Let cool before serving.
8 servings

CHERRY SUPREME

The dark cherries offer a flavorful treat.

Crust:

1/2 cup butter or margarine
1 cup all-purpose flour

1/4 cup sugar
1/2 cup finely chopped pecans

Filling:

1/2 cup sugar
1 package (3 ounces) black
   cherry-flavored gelatin
1 cup hot water
1 package (16 ounces)
   Frozen Stokely's®
   Dark Sweet Cherries

1 cup plain yogurt
1 cup whipping cream,
   whipped

Preheat oven to 350°F. Melt butter in skillet; add flour, sugar, and pecans, mixing well. Press mixture into 8-inch square pan to form a crust. Bake 8 to 10 minutes. Cool.

Filling: Dissolve sugar and gelatin in hot water; chill until egg white consistency. Cut frozen cherries in half while still frozen. Add cherries to chilled gelatin. Fold in yogurt and whipped cream. Spoon into prepared crust; chill until firm.   *6 servings*

FLUFFY ANGEL PIE

Truly "angel-like" and great.

Crust:

1 1/4 cups graham cracker
   crumbs (15 graham
   crackers)

3 Tablespoons sugar
1/3 cup butter or margarine,
   melted

Filling:

1 cup evaporated milk
1 package (3 ounces)
   orange-flavored gelatin
1/2 cup sugar
1 cup boiling water
1/3 cup plus 2 Tablespoons
   orange juice, divided

1 teaspoon grated orange
   rind
1 can (17 ounces)
   Stokely's Finest®
   Fruit Cocktail,
   well drained

Preheat oven to 325°F. Combine graham cracker crumbs with sugar and butter. Line sides and bottom of 9-inch pie plate with crumbs. Bake 7 to 8 minutes. Cool. Place evaporated milk in mixing bowl in freezer, along with beaters, and freeze until soft crystals form around edge of milk (20 to 25 minutes). Dissolve gelatin and sugar in boiling water. Add 1/3 cup orange juice and orange rind. Place in refrigerator and chill until the consistency of unbeaten egg whites. Remove evaporated milk from freezer and whip until stiff; add reserved 2 Tablespoons orange juice and whip until very stiff. Fold in chilled gelatin mixture and well-drained fruit cocktail. Spoon into cooled crust. Chill until firm (3 to 4 hours).   *6 to 8 servings*

Nice to know: Use your blender or food processor to make cracker crumbs quickly and easily.

GRASSHOPPER PEAR PIE

A perennial favorite.

1/4 cup butter or margarine, melted	1 can (16 ounces) Stokely's Finest® Sliced Bartlett Pears, well drained
1 1/2 cups chocolate cookie crumbs (39 chocolate wafers)	1/4 cup crème de menthe
26 marshmallows	1 cup whipping cream, whipped
3/4 cup milk	

Preheat oven to 350°F. Combine butter and cookie crumbs. Press firmly into 9-inch pie plate and bake 8 minutes. Cool. Meanwhile, heat marshmallows and milk over medium heat until marshmallows are melted. Cool until mixture is thickened but not set. Dice pears and place in cooled crust. Add crème de menthe to marshmallow mixture. Fold in whipped cream. Pour over pears and refrigerate until firm, 4 hours or overnight.   *8 servings*

Microwave Method: Melt butter in microwave oven. Combine butter and crumbs and press firmly into 9-inch pie plate. Microcook 2 minutes, rotating pie plate 1/2 turn after 1 minute. Cool. Place marshmallows and milk in 2-quart casserole. Microcook 4 minutes or until marshmallows are melted, stirring after 2 minutes. Cool until mixture is thickened but not set. Dice pears and place in cooled crust. Add crème de menthe to marshmallow mixture. Fold in whipped cream. Pour over pears and refrigerate until firm, 4 hours or overnight.

SPICY APPLESAUCE
ICE CREAM ROLL

Easy — and makes a great impression.

3 eggs	1 teaspoon cinnamon, divided
1 cup sugar	
1 can (16 1/2 ounces)	1/4 teaspoon nutmeg
Stokely's Finest®	1/4 teaspoon salt
Applesauce, divided	Confectioners sugar
1 cup all-purpose flour	1 quart vanilla ice cream,
1 teaspoon baking powder	slightly softened

Preheat oven to 375°F. Line greased 15×10×1-inch jelly-roll pan with waxed paper; grease paper. In small mixing bowl, beat eggs at high speed with electric mixer 5 minutes. Gradually beat in sugar and 1/2 cup applesauce (reserving remaining applesauce for topping). Sift together flour, baking powder, 3/4 teaspoon cinnamon, nutmeg, and salt; blend into egg mixture using low speed of mixer. Spread batter in prepared pan and bake 15 minutes, or until cake is lightly browned and springs back when pressed with finger. Sprinkle clean dish towel with confectioners sugar. Immediately invert cake onto prepared towel. Remove waxed paper; roll cake and towel from narrow end; cool completely. Unroll cake, trim edges if desired, remove from towel, spread with softened ice cream, and reroll. Wrap tightly in foil or plastic film and freeze. Blend reserved applesauce with remaining 1/4 teaspoon cinnamon; chill. When ready to serve, cut roll into 8 or 10 slices. Top each slice with applesauce mixture.   *8 to 10 servings*

Opposite: Spicy Applesauce Ice Cream Roll

OLD FASHIONED RHUBARB PIE

Just like Grandma used to make.

2 eggs, beaten
2 Tablespoons milk
1 1/2 cups sugar
6 Tablespoons all-purpose
   flour
1/4 teaspoon salt
1/4 teaspoon nutmeg

1 package (20 ounces)
   Frozen Stokely's®
   Cut Rhubarb
Pastry for 9-inch pie
   shell and lattice top
1 Tablespoon butter or
   margarine

Preheat oven to 400°F. Combine eggs with milk, sugar, flour, salt, and nutmeg in large bowl; mix with rhubarb. Pour into unbaked pie shell and dot with butter. Cover with lattice top. Bake 50 to 60 minutes, or until rhubarb is tender and crust is golden brown.
6 servings

CHEESEY PUMPKIN PIE

A surprise layer inside.

2 packages (3 ounces each)
   cream cheese, softened
1/4 cup sugar
1/2 teaspoon vanilla
   extract
2 eggs (used separately)

1 9-inch pie shell,
   unbaked
1 can (18 ounces)
   Stokely's Finest®
   Pumpkin Pie Filling
1 cup evaporated milk

Blend cream cheese, sugar, and vanilla at medium speed of electric mixer or in food processor until smooth. Add 1 egg and mix well. Pour into unbaked pie shell and refrigerate 1 hour. Meanwhile, preheat oven to 450°F. Combine remaining egg, pumpkin pie filling, and evaporated milk. Carefully spoon pumpkin mixture over cream cheese layer. Bake 10 minutes. Reduce heat to 350°F. and continue baking 60 minutes, or until knife inserted in center comes out clean.   *8 servings*

Recipe Ingredient Equivalents

1 stick butter (1/4 pound)	1/2 cup
1 square chocolate	1 ounce
16 ounces (1 pound) process cheese	4 cups shredded cheese
4 ounces (1/4 pound) process cheese	1 cup shredded cheese
1 pound brown sugar	2 1/4 cups firmly packed
1 pound confectioners sugar	3 1/3 cups
1 pound flour	4 1/2 cups sifted
9 graham crackers, coarsely crushed	1 cup crumbs
11 graham crackers, finely crushed	1 cup crumbs
1 cup dry bread crumbs	3 slices bread
1 cup soft bread crumbs	1 1/4 slices bread
1 cup uncooked rice	3 1/2 to 4 cups cooked rice
1 cup precooked rice	2 1/2 to 3 cups prepared rice
8 ounces uncooked egg noodles	4 cups cooked noodles
8 ounces uncooked spaghetti	5 cups cooked spaghetti
8 ounces (2 cups) uncooked elbow macaroni	4 1/2 cups cooked macaroni
1 medium-size onion, chopped	1/2 cup
1/4 pound celery (2 stalks), chopped	1 cup
1 pound fresh mushrooms	1 can (6 ounces) canned
1 lemon	2 1/2 to 3 Tablespoons juice
1 orange	6 to 7 Tablespoons juice
12 to 14 egg yolks	1 cup
8 to 10 egg whites	1 cup

Recipe Ingredient Substitutions

1 cup cake flour	1 cup sifted all-purpose flour less 2 Tablespoons
1 Tablespoon cornstarch	2 Tablespoons flour
1 teaspoon baking powder	1/4 teaspoon baking soda plus 1/2 teaspoon cream of tartar or
	1/4 teaspoon baking soda plus 1/2 cup sour milk to replace 1/2 cup liquid in recipe
1/2 cup margarine or butter	1/2 cup shortening plus 1/2 teaspoon salt
1 cup whole milk	1/2 cup evaporated milk plus 1/2 cup water or 1 cup reconstituted nonfat dry milk plus 2 teaspoons butter
1 cup sour milk or buttermilk	1 Tablespoon lemon juice or vinegar plus sweet whole milk to make 1 cup; let stand 5 minutes
1 cup yogurt	1 cup buttermilk
1 square unsweetened chocolate	3 Tablespoons cocoa plus 1 Tablespoon margarine or butter
1 cup molasses	1 cup honey
1 cup honey	3/4 cup sugar plus 1/4 cup liquid
1 Tablespoon fresh snipped herbs	1 teaspoon dried herbs
1 small fresh onion	1 Tablespoon instant minced onion, rehydrated
1 small clove garlic	1/8 teaspoon garlic powder
1 teaspoon dry mustard	1 Tablespoon prepared mustard

Index

A Skettee Weenee Meal, 34
Accompaniments
Eastern Beans, 97
German-Style Hominy, 122
Golden Hominy Parmesan, 121
Hawaiian Pork and Beans, 94
Hominy au Gratin, 120
Hominy Olé, 113
Mom's Baked Beans, 100
Ranch House Beans, 91
Sour Cream Frijoles, 93
Almond-Chocolate Coated Pears, 170
Aloha Skillet Hominy, 69
Appetizers
Cheese Filled Beets, 8
Hot Bean Dip, 11
Meatballs in Red Wine Sauce, 12
Melon Balls on Ice, 9
Miniature Chicken Egg Foo Yung, 7
Pimiento Cheese Spread, 9
Spinach Balls, 11
Spinach-Cheese Spread, 8
Appetizing Kraut, 65
Apple-Kraut Bavarian, 61
Apple-Sausage Skillet, 73
Applesauce Bars, 169
Applesauce Flip, 12
Applesauce Fruit Cake, 157
Apricot Bean Casserole, 56
Asparagus Luncheon, 86
Asparagus Vinaigrette, 129
Asparagus with Golden Fruit Sauce, 117

Baked Fruit Sauce, 142
Baked Popcorn Crunch, 16
Barbecued Beef, 32
Barbecued Green Beans, 89
Basic Syrup for Popcorn, 149
Bayou Pan Dinner, 93
Bean Tacos, 66
Beans and Franks, 64
Beef
Barbecued Beef, 32
Beef Chop Suey, 49
Beef in a Packet, 46
Beef Parmigiana, 52
Beef Stew Three Ways, 38
Biscuit-Topped Beef 'N Beans, 36
Cantonese Flank Steak, 51
Chuckwagon Pepper Steak, 44
Colonial Pot Roast, 46
Corn O'Plenty, 39
Corn-Stuffed Round Steak, 56
Corny Beef Casserole, 48
Crunchy Beef and Shellie Beans, 45
Fiesta Meatball Supper, 37
Kraut 'N Burger Balls, 55
Meatballs in Red Wine Sauce, 12
Mexican Pie, 36
Mozzarella Meat Loaf, 52
Pressure Cooker Roast, 48

Rouladen, 55
Skillet Goulash, 39
Slow-Cooked Boiled Dinner, 49
Smothered Steaks, 45
Sombrero Pie, 42
Spanish Stuffed Peppers, 42
Stuffed Beef Rolls with Sherried
Asparagus Sauce, 54
Swedish Cabbage Rolls, 35
Swiss Steak and Vegetables, 44
Texas Chili, 41
Texas-Style Beef and Beans, 43
Vegetable Pie, 57
Beef Chop Suey, 49
Beef in a Packet, 46
Beef Parmigiana, 52
Beef Stew Three Ways, 38
Beet Conserve, 142
Beet-Pineapple Salad, 140
Beverages
Applesauce Flip, 12
Frothy Nectar, 13
Melon "Ice Ring" Punch, 18
Strawberry Mocha Shake, 13
Trigo Shake, 13
Biscuit-Topped Beef 'N Beans, 36
Black Forest Cherry Cake, 156
Blueberry Crisp, 171
Blueberry Muffins, 143
Bordelaise Sauce, 149
Breads and Muffins
Blueberry Muffins, 143
Corn Muffins, 148
Mexican Corn Bread, 143
Orangey Pumpkin Bread, 147
Broccoli Cheese Casserole, 91
Broccoli-Chicken Quiche, 141
Broccoli Roll-Ups, 72
Broccoli Spears with Mustard Sauce, 134
Brussels Sprouts Royal, 123
Butter Bean Chicken Casserole, 81
Butter Bean Soup, 27
Butter Crisp Topping, 153

Cakes
Applesauce Fruit Cake, 157
Black Forest Cherry Cake, 156
Carrot Cake, 159
Choco-Moist Cake, 156
Chocolate Kraut Cake, 160
Fruit Cocktail Cake, 158
Gum Drop Cake, 155
Pear Upside Down Cake, 161
Quick and Easy Strawberry
Shortcake, 161
Spicy Applesauce Ice Cream Roll, 182
Strawberry Sour Cream Bundt Cake, 158
Candied Popcorn Ornaments, 152
Cannelloni Supreme, 78
Cantonese Flank Steak, 51

Carrot Cake, 159
Carrot Casserole, 93
Carrot Soup, 21
Casserole Milano, 59
Casseroles
  Apricot Bean Casserole, 56
  Beans and Franks, 64
  Biscuit-Topped Beef 'N Beans, 36
  Broccoli Cheese Casserole, 91
  Butter Bean Chicken Casserole, 81
  Carrot Casserole, 93
  Casserole Milano, 59
  Chinese Green Bean Casserole, 92
  Chorizo Casserole, 60
  Company Vegetable Casserole, 90
  Corny Beef Casserole, 48
  Country-Style Sauerkraut and
    Sausages, 70
  Crunchy Chicken Casserole, 77
  Easy Barbecue Chicken Casserole, 83
  Easy Fish Casserole, 87
  Fruity Bean Bake, 104
  German Pork and Bean Bake, 65
  Kraut-Dog Bake, 64
  Next Day Casserole, 79
  Noodlee Weenee Surprises, 34
  Parisian Dinner, 72
  Peachy Bean Casserole, 57
  Pinwheel Sausage Bake, 68
  Plan-Over Turkey Casserole, 77
  Saucy Chicken Casserole, 82
  Sauerkraut Bake, 123
  Sauerkraut-Noodle Bake, 96
  Seaside Casserole, 88
  Three Bean Bake, 109
Cauliflower Caper, 136
Cheddar Zucchini Supreme, 90
Cheese
  Broccoli-Chicken Quiche, 141
  Cheese Filled Beets, 8
  Green Bean and Smoked
    Cheese Combo, 101
  Lasagna, 53
  Pimiento Cheese Spread, 9
  Spinach-Cheese Spread, 8
Cheese Filled Beets, 8
Cheesy Cauliflower and Peas, 114
Cheesy Pumpkin Pie, 184
Cherry Supreme, 180
Chicken à la King, 80
Chicken and Shrimp Royale, 85
Chicken Breasts Supreme, 75
Chicken 'N Peaches Polynesian, 78
Chicken Orient with Cashews, 81
Chiffon Strawberry Pie, 178
Chili Beef Onion Soup, 22
Chinese Chicken with Cherries, 84
Chinese Green Bean Casserole, 92
Choco-Moist Cake, 156
Choco-Peanut Butter Chews, 14
Chocolate Cream Cheese Frosting, 160
Chocolate Kraut Cake, 160

Chorizo Casserole, 60
Chuckwagon Pepper Steak, 44
Coffee Peach Parfait, 169
Colonial Pot Roast, 46
Company Vegetable Casserole, 90
Confetti Beans Parmesan, 102
Cool Corn Salad, 129
Corn Bread Topping, 60
Corn Chowder, 24
Corn Flapjacks, 148
Corn Muffins, 148
Corn O'Plenty, 39
Corn Pudding, 92
Corn-Stuffed Round Steak, 56
Corny Beef Casserole, 48
Corny-Chicken Salad, 125
Country-Style Sauerkraut and Sausages, 70
Cranberry Beets, 115
Cream Cheese Frosting, 159
Creamed Spinach Ring, 97
Creamed Vegetable Soup, 25
Creole Skillet, 94
Creole-Style Green Beans, 108
Crêpe Sandwich Torte, 33
Crêpes, Strawberry, 172
Crispy Caramel Corn, 17
Crispy Chicken with Peach Cups, 76
Crock-Cooked Vegetable Beef
  Soup, 22
Crunchy Beef and Shellie Beans, 45
Crunchy Chicken Casserole, 77

Decorated Popcorn Wreath, 152
Deep-Fried Vegetable Medley, 96
Del Sol Vinaigrette, 133
Desserts
  Cherry Supreme, 180
  Coffee Peach Parfaits, 169
  Flaming Cherries Jubilee, 164
  Peach Bavarian Cream, 163
  Peach Pizza, 172
  Rhubarb Crisp, 173
  Scotchy Peach Sundaes, 177
  Strawberry Crêpes, 172
  Strawberry-Peach Trifle, 171
Devilish Brussels Sprouts, 105
Dill Sauced Peas, 108
Dilly-Cauliflower Soup, 21
Double Bean Soup Italian, 20

Eastern Beans, 97
Easy Barbecue Chicken Casserole, 83
Easy Cherry Pudding, 168
Easy Fish Casserole, 87
Easy Spinach, 121
Eggs
  Gypsy Scramble, 154
  Miniature Chicken Egg Foo Yung, 7
  Ranch-Style Eggs, 154
  Tropical Omelet, 145
Elegant Wax Beans Parmesan, 104

Favorite Lima Barbecue, 114
Fiesta Chicken Salad, 131
Fiesta Meatball Supper, 37
Flaming Cheeries Jubilee with Ice Cream, 164
Florentine Submarines, 30
Florentine Vegetables with
    Shrimp Sauce, 109
Fluffy Angel Pie, 180
Frostings
    Caramel Frosting, 169
    Chocolate Cream Cheese Frosting, 160
    Cream Cheese Frosting, 159
Frothy Nectar, 13
Frozen Fruit Salad, 138
Frozen Vegetables Cooked in a Packet, 106
Fruit
    Almond-Chocolate Coated Pears, 170
    Macaroon Peaches, 175
    Melon Balls on Ice, 9
    Peach Clouds, 164
    Peach Hay Stacks, 163
    Peaches Southern Style, 168
    Sherried Fruit Compote, 174
    Top Hat Pears, 170
    Warm Fruitful Compote, 166
Fruit Cocktail Cake, 158
Fruitful Tarts with Orange
    Glacé, 174
Fruity Bean Bake, 104

Gatorade Popsicles, 16
Gelatin Molds
    Beet-Pineapple Salad, 140
    Grapefruit Velvet Fluff, 138
    Green Bean Crunchies with
        Tangy Dressing, 132
    Nutty Beet Salad, 133
    Pink Applesauce Salad, 139
    Royal Pear Salad, 136
    Spring Fluff, 165
    Surprise Salad, 134
German Pork and Bean Bake, 65
German-Style Hominy, 122
Glazed Carrots, 112
Glazed Pork Chops, 68
Golden Hominy Parmesan, 121
Golden Nugget Pie, 178
Goldenrod Green Beans, 123
Grapefruit Velvet Fluff, 138
Grasshopper Pear Pie, 181
Green Bean and Smoked
    Cheese Combo, 101
Green Bean Crunchies with Tangy
    Dressing, 132
Green Bean Divan, 75
Green Beans with Bacon Dressing, 120
Gum Drop Cake, 155
Gypsy Scramble, 154

Hamburger Vegetable Soup, 20
Hawaiian Pork and Beans, 94
Home-Style Vegetable Soup, 25

Hominy Olé, 113
Hominy au Gratin, 120
Honeyed Beets, 112
Hot Bean Dip, 11
Hot Chicken Cocktail Salad, 84
Hot Diggety Dog Skillet, 61
Hot Milano Salad, 118
Hot Tuna Sandwiches, 32

Iced Sweet Cherry Soup, 28
Italian Skillet, 67

Japanese Stir-Fry Pork, 71
Jiffy Lunch, 34

Kraut-Dog Bake, 64
Kraut 'N Burger Balls, 55
Kraut 'N Chop Bake, 62
Kraut Relish, 139

Large Christmas Tree, 153
Lasagna, 53

Macaroon Peaches, 175
Make Ahead Cauliflower Salad, 135
Mama's Southern Green Beans, 115
Meatballs in Red Wine Sauce, 12
Melon Balls on Ice, 9
Melon "Ice Ring" Punch, 18
Mexican Corn Bread, 143
Mexican Pie, 36
Microwave Recipes
    Baked Fruit Sauce, 142
    Barbecued Beef, 32
    Barbecued Green Beans, 89
    Beet Conserve, 142
    Butter Bean Soup, 27
    Casserole Milano, 59
    Chili Beef Onion Soup, 22
    Corn Pudding, 92
    Creole Skillet, 94
    Double Bean Soup Italian, 20
    Fiesta Meatball Supper, 37
    Grasshopper Pear Pie, 181
    Green Beans with Bacon Dressing, 120
    Hot Bean Dip, 11
    New England Lima Bean Bake, 110
    Next Day Casserole, 79
    Parisian Dinner, 72
    Pea Soup, 24
    Plan-Over Turkey Casserole, 77
    Saucy Beets, 101
    Spanish Corn and Zucchini, 100
    Spanish Stuffed Peppers, 42
    Texas Chili, 41
    Vegetables, Canned and Frozen, 106
    Warm Fruitful Compote, 166
    Zippy Pork and Beans, 74
Mid-East Curried Pork Sandwiches, 29
Milano Medley, 99
Miniature Chicken Egg Foo Yung, 7
Mom's Baked Beans, 100

Mom's Delectable Chicken, 82
Mozzarella Meat Loaf, 52

Natural Munch, 14
New England Lima Bean Bake, 110
New Orleans Bean Salad, 128
Next Day Casserole, 79
Noodlee Weenee Surprises, 34
Nutty Acorn Beans, 102
Nutty Beet Salad, 133
Nutty Broccoli Salad, 29

Old Fashioned Rhubarb Pie, 184
Orange Glazed Beets, 113
Oranged Parisian Vegetables, 119
Orange Shell Squash, 124
Orangey Pork and Beans, 61
Orangey Pumpkin Bread, 147
Oriental Soup, 19
Oven Chicken Stew, 76

Parisian Dinner, 72
Parisian Soufflé Roll-Up, 70
Pasta and Rice
Bayou Pan Dinner, 93
Hot Diggety Dog Skillet, 61
Lasagna, 53
Pinwheel Sausage Bake, 68
Saucy Chicken Casserole, 82
Sauerkraut-Noodle Bake, 96
Skillet Goulash, 39
Skillet Rice Supper, 69
Smothered Steaks, 45
Swedish Cabbage Rolls, 35
Pea Salad, 134
Pea Soup, 24
Peach Bavarian Cream, 163
Peach Clouds, 164
Peach Hay Stacks, 163
Peach Kuchen, 165
Peach Pizza, 172
Peaches Southern Style, 168
Peachy Bean Casserole, 57
Pear Crunch Pie, 177
Pear Upside Down Cake, 161
Peas à la Crème, 110
Peas 'N Salmon Loaf, 87
Peas with Maple Syrup, 113
Pecan Chicken 'N Broccoli, 83
Pies, Dessert
Cheesy Pumpkin Pie, 184
Chiffon Strawberry Pie, 178
Fluffy Angel Pie, 180
Fruitful Tarts with Orange Glacé, 174
Golden Nugget Pie, 178
Grasshopper Pear Pie, 181
Old Fashioned Rhubarb Pie, 184
Pear Crunch Pie, 177
Pumpkin Pecan Pie, 179
Sour Cream Pumpkin Pie, 179
Pies, Main Dish
Broccoli-Chicken Quiche, 141
Chicken a la King, 80

Mexican Pie, 36
Sombrero Pie, 42
Tamale Bean Pie, 60
Vegetable Pie, 57
Pimiento Cheese Spread, 9
Pink Applesauce Salad, 139
Pinwheel Sausage Bake, 68
Piquant Vegetable Combo, 116
Plan-Over Turkey Casserole, 77
Popcorn Garland, 152
Popcorn Snowman, 150
Pork
Broccoli Roll-Ups, 72
Cannelloni Supreme, 78
Glazed Pork Chops, 68
Japanese Stir-Fry Pork, 71
Kraut 'N Chop Bake, 62
Orangey Pork and Beans, 61
Pork and Peaches Chinese Style, 66
Pork Chops and Peas with
  Mushroom Sauce, 67
Rouladen, 55
Sauerkraut and Spareribs, 74
Soup-erb Broccoli and Ham, 28
Pork and Peaches Chinese Style, 66
Pork Chops and Peas with Mushroom
  Sauce, 67
Poultry
Butter Bean Chicken Casserole, 81
Cannelloni Supreme, 78
Chicken à la King, 80
Chicken and Shrimp Royale, 85
Chicken Breasts Supreme, 75
Chicken 'N Peaches Polynesian, 78
Chicken Orient with Cashews, 81
Chinese Chicken with Cherries, 84
Corny-Chicken Salad, 125
Crispy Chicken with Peach Cups, 76
Crunchy Chicken Casserole, 77
Easy Barbecue Chicken Casserole, 83
Fiesta Chicken Salad, 131
Green Bean Divan, 75
Hot Chicken Cocktail Salad, 84
Mom's Delectable Chicken, 82
Next Day Casserole, 79
Nutty Broccoli Salad, 29
Oven Chicken Stew, 76
Pecan Chicken 'N Broccoli, 83
Plan-Over Turkey Casserole, 77
Saucy Chicken Casserole, 82
Pressure Cooker Dishes
Beef Stew Three Ways, 38
Pressure Cooker Roast, 48
Pressure Cooker Roast, 48
Puddings
Corn Pudding, 92
Easy Cherry Pudding, 168
Peach Clouds, 164
Peach Kuchen, 165
Pumpkin Rumkins, 175
Puffy Corn Fritters, 147
Pumpkin Pecan Pie, 179
Pumpkin Rumkins, 175

Quick and Easy Strawberry Shortcake, 161
Quick Chilee Weenee Tacos, 27
Quick Corn Relish, 140

Raisin-Pineapple Beets, 117
Ranch House Beans, 91
Ranch-Style Eggs, 154
Recipe Ingredient Equivalents, 185
Recipe Ingredient Substitutions, 186
Red Bean Salad, 135
Refreshing Corn Salad, 139
Relishes and Conserves
  Beet Conserve, 142
  Kraut Relish, 139
  Quick Corn Relish, 140
Reuben Sandwiches, 30
Rhubarb Crisp, 173
Rouladen, 55
Royal Pear Salad, 136

Salad Romano, 132
Salads
  Asparagus Vinaigrette, 129
  Broccoli Spears with Mustard Sauce, 134
  Cauliflower Caper, 136
  Cool Corn Salad, 129
  Corny-Chicken Salad, 125
  Del Sol Vinaigrette, 133
  Fiesta Chicken Salad, 131
  Frozen Fruit Salad, 138
  Hot Milano Salad, 118
  Make Ahead Cauliflower Salad, 135
  New Orleans Bean Salad, 128
  Nutty Broccoli Salad, 29
  Pea Salad, 134
  Red Bean Salad, 135
  Refreshing Corn Salad, 139
  Salad Romano, 132
  Sauerkraut Salad, 128
  Shrimp Salad Parisian, 88
  Tangy Bean Salad, 131
  Uncommon Salad, 126
  Vegetable Pepperoni Salad, 126
Sandwiches
  Asparagus Luncheon, 86
  Barbecued Beef, 32
  Crêpe Sandwich Torte, 33
  Florentine Submarines, 30
  Hot Tuna Sandwiches, 32
  Mid-East Curried Pork Sandwiches, 29
  Quick Chilee Weenee Tacos, 27
  Reuben Sandwiches, 30
  Soup-erb Broccoli and Ham, 28
Sauced Wax Beans, 122
Sauces and Dressings
  Baked Fruit Sauce, 142
  Basic Syrup for Popcorn, 149
  Bordelaise Sauce, 149
  Sour Cream-Mustard Sauce, 33
  Superb French Salad Dressing, 128
  Tangy Dressing, 132
Saucy Beets, 101

Saucy Chicken Casserole, 82
Sauerkraut and Spareribs, 74
Sauerkraut Bake, 123
Sauerkraut-Noodle Bake, 96
Sauerkraut Salad, 128
Sausages
  Aloha Skillet Hominy, 69
  Appetizing Kraut, 65
  Apple-Kraut Bavarian, 61
  Apple-Sausage Skillet, 73
  Bean Tacos, 66
  Beans and Franks, 64
  Chorizo Casserole, 60
  Country-Style Sauerkraut and
    Sausages, 70
  German Pork and Bean Bake, 65
  Hot Diggety Dog Skillet, 61
  Italian Skillet, 67
  Kraut-Dog Bake, 64
  Parisian Dinner, 72
  Pinwheel Sausage Bake, 68
  Skillet Rice Supper, 69
  Smoked Sausage Dinner, 73
  Tamale Bean Pie, 60
  Tote Along Bean Bundles, 64
  Zippy Pork and Beans, 74
Savory Lima Beans, 119
Scotchy Peach Sundaes, 177
Seafood
  Chicken and Shrimp Royale, 85
  Easy Fish Casserole, 87
  Peas 'N Salmon Loaf, 87
  Seaside Casserole, 88
  Shrimp Salad Parisian, 88
  Tuna Japanese, 86
  Uncommon Salad, 126
Seaside Casserole, 88
Sherried Fruit Compote, 174
Shrimp Salad Parisian, 88
Skillet Goulash, 39
Skillet Rice Supper, 69
Slow-Cooked Boiled Dinner, 49
Slow Cooker Dishes
  Beef Stew Three Ways, 38
  Crock-Cooked Vegetable Beef Soup, 22
  Kraut 'N Chop Bake, 62
  Mama's Southern Green Beans, 115
  Sauerkraut and Spareribs, 74
  Slow-Cooked Boiled Dinner, 49
Smoked Sausage Dinner, 73
Smothered Steaks, 45
Snacks
  Applesauce Bars, 169
  Baked Popcorn Crunch, 16
  Blueberry Crisp, 171
  Candied Popcorn Ornaments, 152
  Choco-Peanut Butter Chews, 14
  Crispy Caramel Corn, 17
  Decorated Popcorn Wreath, 152
  Gatorade Popsicles, 16
  Large Christmas Tree, 153
  Natural Munch, 14

Popcorn Garland, 152
Popcorn Snowman, 150
Spun Pink-Cinnamon Popcorn, 17
Sugar and Spice Popcorn, 16
Sombrero Pie, 42
Soup-erb Broccoli and Ham, 28
Soups
  Butter Bean Soup, 27
  Carrot Soup, 21
  Chili Beef Onion Soup, 22
  Corn Chowder, 24
  Creamed Vegetable Soup, 25
  Crock-Cooked Vegetable Beef Soup, 22
  Dilly-Cauliflower Soup, 21
  Double Bean Soup Italian, 20
  Hamburger Vegetable Soup, 20
  Home-Style Vegetable Soup, 25
  Iced Sweet Cherry Soup, 28
  Oriental Soup, 19
  Pea Soup, 24
Sour Cream Frijoles, 93
Sour Cream-Mustard Sauce, 33
Sour Cream Pumpkin Pie, 179
Spanish Corn and Zucchini, 100
Spanish Stuffed Peppers, 42
Spicy Applesauce Ice Cream Roll, 182
Spinach Balls, 11
Spinach-Cheese Spread, 8
Spinach-Zucchini Boats, 116
Spring Fluff, 165
Sprouts Amandine, 115
Spun Pink-Cinnamon Popcorn, 17
Strawberry Crêpes, 172
Strawberry Mocha Shake, 13
Strawberry-Peach Trifle, 171
Strawberry Sour Cream Bundt Cake, 158
Stuffed Beef Rolls with Sherried
  Asparagus Sauce, 54
Sugar and Spice Popcorn, 16
Superb French Salad Dressing, 128
Surprise Salad, 134
Swedish Cabbage Rolls, 35
Sweet 'N Sour Cantonese, 105
Sweet Peas and Carrots, 112
Sweet-Sour Shellie Beans, 124
Sweetened Sour Cream, 175
Swiss Beans, 118
Swiss Steak and Vegetables, 44

Tamale Bean Pie, 60
Tangy Bean Salad, 131
Texas Chili, 41
Texas-Style Beef and Beans, 43
Three Bean Bake, 109
Top Hat Pears, 170
Toppings
  Butter Crisp Topping, 153
  Corn Bread Topping, 60
  Sweetened Sour Cream, 175
Tote Along Bean Bundles, 64
Trigo Shake, 13
Tropical Omelet, 145
Tuna Japanese, 86

Uncommon Salad, 126

Vegetable Pepperoni Salad, 126
Vegetable Pie, 57
Vegetables
  Asparagus with Golden Fruit Sauce, 117
  Barbecued Green Beans, 89
  Bayou Pan Dinner, 93
  Brussels Sprouts Royal, 123
  Cheesy Cauliflower and Peas, 114
  Confetti Beans Parmesan, 102
  Cooking, Canned and Frozen, 106, 107
  Cranberry Beets, 115
  Creamed Spinach Ring, 97
  Creole Skillet, 94
  Creole-Style Green Beans, 108
  Deep-Fried Vegetable Medley, 96
  Devilish Brussels Sprouts, 105
  Dill Sauced Peas, 108
  Easy Spinach, 121
  Elegant Wax Beans Parmesan, 104
  Favorite Lima Barbecue, 114
  Florentine Vegetables with
    Shrimp Sauce, 109
  Frozen Vegetables in a Packet, 106
  Glazed Carrots, 112
  Goldenrod Green Beans, 123
  Green Bean and Smoked
    Cheese Combo, 101
  Green Beans with Bacon Dresssing, 120
  Honeyed Beets, 112
  Mama's Southern Green Beans, 115
  Microwaving vegetables, 106
  Milano Medley, 99
  New England Lima Bean Bake, 110
  Nutty Acorn Beans, 102
  Orange Glazed Beets, 113
  Oranged Parisian Vegetables, 119
  Orange Shell Squash, 124
  Peas à la Crème, 110
  Peas with Maple Syrup, 113
  Piquant Vegetable Combo, 116
  Raisin-Pineapple Beets, 117
  Sauced Wax Beans, 122
  Saucy Beets, 101
  Savory Lima Beans, 119
  Spanish Corn and Zucchini, 100
  Spanish Stuffed Peppers, 42
  Spinach-Zucchini Boats, 116
  Sprouts Amandine, 115
  Sweet 'N Sour Cantonese, 105
  Sweet Peas and Carrots, 112
  Sweet-Sour Shellie Beans, 124
  Swiss Beans, 118
  Three Bean Bake, 109
  Vegetables del Sol in Golden Puff, 99
Vegetables del Sol in Golden Puff, 99

Warm Fruitful Compote, 166

Zippy Pork and Beans, 74